The Monroe Doctrine

By

William Fiddian Reddaway

Published by Forgotten Books 2012

Originally Published 1898

PIBN 1000426515

THE MONROE DOCTRINE

London: C. J. CLAY AND SONS,

CAMBRIDGE UNIVERSITY PRESS WAREHOUSE,

AVE MARIA LANE.

Glasgow: 263, ARGYLE STREET.

Leipzig: F. A. BROCKHAUS.

New York: THE MACMILLAN COMPANY.

Bombay: E. SEYMOUR HALE.

THE MONROE DOCTRINE

BY

W. F. REDDAWAY, B.A.

FELLOW OF KING'S COLLEGE, CAMBRIDGE.

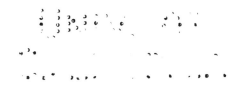

Cambridge:

AT THE UNIVERSITY PRESS.

1898

𝕮𝖆𝖒𝖇𝖗𝖎𝖉𝖌𝖊:

PRINTED BY J. & C. F. CLAY,

AT THE UNIVERSITY PRESS.

PREFACE.

THE following pages are published for the most part in the form in which they were written during the summer of 1896 in competition for the Members' Prize. Some re-arrangement has, however, been made, and in particular Chapter II., describing generally the diplomatic situation in 1823, has been condensed from what was originally a more elaborate examination of those international relations which may be regarded as the remoter causes of the Monroe Doctrine. One of the factors which produced these relations, the group of revolted colonies that may be collectively described as Spanish America, has been separately treated of in an Appendix.

Nothing newly published has seemed to the author to render necessary any modification of the main conclusions of the essay:—that the evolution of the Monroe Doctrine was gradual; that the peculiar form of the Message of 1823 was due to John Quincy Adams; that he, and he alone, logically applied it in politics; and that it produced its desired effect as an act of policy, but in no way modified the Law of Nations. The recent policy of the United States towards both Cuba and Hawaii appears to add strength to the argument of the last chapter—that since 1829 appeals to the Doctrine have been regulated by neither the nature nor the limits of the original.

It is perhaps not too much to say that, while the use of the name 'Monroe Doctrine' serves a purpose in exciting and rendering intelligible to the world a particular American feeling which may be the outcome of legitimate national aspirations, it too often reveals the defects of a formula imperfectly expressed and inappropriately applied. The Monroe Doctrine of current politics, indeed, seems to have become rather an 'Adams sentiment,' changed by the development of circumstances from anything that Adams, as a statesman of the Thirties, can be said to have expressly advocated. The author has therefore chosen to dwell on the evolution and application of the original Doctrine, rather than on the twisted and spasmodic products which have, during the last half-century, been labelled with its name.

Among the published authorities on which the work has been based are the 'Memoirs of John Quincy

Adams,' the various writings of Richard Rush, the biographical works of A. G. and E. J. Stapleton dealing with George Canning, E. T. Williams' 'Statesman's Manual,' the 'American Annual Register,' D. C. Gilman's 'Life of Monroe,' Chateaubriand's 'Congres de Verone,' Senator T. H. Benton's 'Thirty Years' View,' a series of articles in the 'Political Science Quarterly,' a series of despatches and discussions in the 'Times,' W. B. Lawrence's 'Commentaire sur Wheaton,' Professor Bryce's 'American Commonwealth,' Mr Goldwin Smith's 'United States,' and the writings of A. H. Everett. A mass of the unpublished documents in the Public Record Office bearing upon the subject, together with the printed papers which they contain, has also been largely laid under contribution.

I have to express my thanks to Messrs Hubert Hall and A. E. Stamp, of the Public Record Office, for facilitating the production of this essay, to Professor T. E. Holland, Professor Westlake, and Dr Cunningham for their valuable criticism and corrections, and to many friends for their kind suggestions and advice.

W. F. REDDAWAY.

King's College, Cambridge,
January 1898.

THE MONROE DOCTRINE.

INTRODUCTION.

THE closing days of the year 1895 furnished much material worthy the study of the pathologist of democracy. They showed the spectacle of the two most powerful nations of the modern world—nations united by the closest ties of blood, of speech, and of common interest,—standing on the brink of war for a cause that might have been accounted light by patrimonial sovereigns. Weeks, and even months, passed before the ferment was allayed, with the result, as Americans admit, of a paralysis on business and a loss of property in the depreciation of securities that no arithmetic can estimate. The source of all was to be sought in a doctrine, a principle, a precept, formulated as men believed, by a statesman whose authority had ceased seventy years before.

This Monroe Doctrine, then, in defence of which the United States thus showed themselves ready to expend so vast a quantity of blood and treasure, and which has even more recently complicated the question of Arbitration, is a force which calls for the attention of every student of modern international politics. A volcano is ever threatening us, and we must know its size and nature. The United States, Great Britain, Spain, and the States of Spanish America, are the parties whose interests at stake are the greatest. But the whole family of nations is at the same time concerned. The biography of the Doctrine, again, tends more and more nearly to become a history of the foreign policy of the United States. In the New World, far more than in the Old, foreign and home politics are linked together, and to follow either is to study the institutions of Republicanism. Throughout its course, moreover, the Monroe Doctrine has never ceased to raise questions of national independence, of intervention, of the equality of States, of treaties, and of the acquisition of territory, which are at once the most important and the most difficult problems of the International Law of Peace. And whatever be the truth about it, a glance at its history, either from the speculative or from the practical point of view, establishes beyond a doubt its claim to a full chapter in the record of human error.

An examination of the Monroe Doctrine cannot be deemed complete if it does not strive to trace its evolution out of the complex circumstances which preceded it. Its authorship, again, forms a problem of some historical and practical interest. From the investigation of origins it is natural to proceed to a study of the effects, political and legal, which it produced. Recent international controversies have shown the necessity of scrutinising its later history. And lastly an attempt, however imperfect, must be made to estimate its bearing upon the politics of the world.

CHAPTER I.

The Postulates of the Monroe Doctrine.

The Doctrine proclaimed by James Monroe in his presidential Message of December 2, 1823, may be roughly described as a prohibition by the United States of European interference with the political arrangements of the New World. For such a prohibition it is easier to find analogy than exact parallel. Modern Europe, it may be maintained, has its Monroe Doctrine against the Turk, just as ancient Hellas had its Monroe Doctrine against the barbarian. Apart, however, from the fact that nations have been wont to condemn classes of acts dangerous to themselves, it might at first sight seem that the principles of the Monroe Doctrine were independent of the past. In the sense that the words of 1823 were not the outcome of a series of approximations by the President of the United States to the doctrine which they express, this view indeed appears to be the true one. But we must not lose sight of the fact that for forty years the United States had been hastening towards the position that they assumed in 1823, while in their progress it is possible to distinguish several landmarks on the road to the Monroe Doctrine. Both their mental attitude and its expression in words become intelligible in the light of previous history.

The self-assertiveness and ambition of the men who threw off the yoke of Laud descended after four generations to the fathers of American independence. At the outbreak of the Seven Years' War the thirteen British Colonies, diverse in origin, in religion, and in interests, had formed a mere strip of territory on the Atlantic seaboard,—a strip hemmed in and dwarfed by huge provinces of France and Spain. At the peace of 1763, however, Canada, Florida and the Mississippi frontier became British, while the remaining French possessions in North America passed under the sovereignty of Spain. The English colonies, therefore, had no longer a formidable rival on their frontiers, and sixteen years later they fulfilled the prophecies of foreign statesmen by their revolt.

During three campaigns France looked on while the British generals failed to deal the decisive blow. Then, as her own writers and statesmen have avowed, she seized the opportunity to humble her ancient rival, and threw the weight of Spain also into the scale of revolution. Four more campaigns were needed, and then—forty years before the Monroe Doctrine—the Americans, bankrupt and exhausted, found themselves struggling with the support of England against the Bourbon monarchs for the line of the Mississippi. "It is impossible," says Mr Lecky, "not to be struck with the skill, hardihood, and good fortune that marked the American negotiations. Everything the United States could, with any shadow of plausibility, demand from England they obtained, and much of what they obtained was granted them in opposition to the two great Powers by whose assistance they had triumphed."

At Versailles, then, the doctrine that even the east coast of North America was closed to European colonisation would have flowed with strange grace from the lips of Franklin or the pen of Washington. In the darkest hours of Valley Forge, however, men in authority had shown something of the buoyant spirit which inspired their successors to declare that the gates of the New World were shut against the politics of the Old. Congress, though powerless to furnish men or money, was never weary of requesting the Commander-in-Chief to conquer Canada. Lafayette, whose imagination prompted him to attack India as well, was saved only by his affection for Washington from attempting the improbable at the bidding of these military theorists. Unable to hold New York, they were burning to hoist the American flag amid the sands of Florida. It even seemed at variance with the new-born continental destiny that the West Indies should own the sway of Britain. These visions, indeed, were hardly more likely to expand the boundaries of the United States than was the grave demonstration of Franklin that England, still mistress of New York, should cede Canada to atone for the damage done by her troops during the war. Like the Doctrine of 1823, they were due to a transcendent national self-confidence, itself the product of the miracles already achieved. Thirteen colonies of the most diverse origin, climate, and institutions, had belied the predictions of the world by joining together in a common cause. A new force had arisen, and that a force unhampered by the neighbourhood of other forces like itself. Having vanquished internal opposition, it had frustrated the most strenuous efforts of the British king. Such success, stimulating men whose powers of speculative thought had brought the quarrel to the test of arms, turned logicians into seers, and gave expression to the belief that Canada and Nova Scotia must soon be members of a Union destined to spread over the northern part of that whole quarter of the globe. The immediate practical effect of aspirations bounded only by the ocean was seen in the tenacity with which the Americans clung to the Mississippi frontier. When peace was signed they rejoiced in the acknowledgment of a title to perhaps a fifth part of habitable North America. Of knowledge of their hemisphere to the west and south of the Mississippi, still less of influence or authority over it, they possessed scarcely a trace.

The history of the four decades which followed the Peace of Versailles is the story of how the Monroe Doctrine became possible. After six years of exhaustion and anarchy, the colonies achieved a government, and by the exchange of Ministers with European Powers, prepared to inaugurate a foreign policy. Their population steadily rose. Less than four millions in 1790, it had increased by a constant ratio to more than ten millions in 1823. Successive Presidents, whether Gallican or Anglican, Republican or Federalist, united in seizing every opportunity to enlarge their boundaries. Settlement to the west of the Alleghanies pursued an unbroken course, and in 1803 the Federal area was doubled by the purchase of Louisiana from Napoleon. France thus once more consented to her own obliteration from the map of North America. She left the United States hedged in by the territories of Great Britain and Spain, and by the unexplored country of Oregon.

Standing midway between the achievement of independence by the United States and the swelling declaration of 1823, the acquisition of Louisiana forms a landmark on the road to the Monroe Doctrine. In common with the growth of internal communication, it promoted the national cohesion of the Federation suddenly called upon to rule an empire. Among its more tangible results were titles, though doubtful ones, to the Oregon district and to the western portion of Florida. The former, indeed, could present no immediate attractions to the United States, but the maritime value of the Floridas, now cut off from the great mass of Spanish dominions, had not failed to arouse their attention. The tide of circumstances ran strongly in their favour. In 1809, when the Presidency of Madison began, Spain found herself so paralysed in Europe that she could hardly lift a finger to prevent her New World dominions from throwing off her yoke. Great Britain, whose representative at Washington could say to the Secretary of State with the approval of his Government, " Such are the ties by which His Majesty is bound to Spain that he cannot see with indifference any attack upon her interest in America," was forbidden by her strained relations with the United States from maintaining by diplomacy, and by her struggle with Napoleon from maintaining by force that guarantee of Spanish possessions to which Spain appealed. The United States, therefore, enjoyed perfect

freedom of action in their dealings with West Florida,
and a curious prototype of the Monroe Doctrine was the
result.

On the 1st November, 1810, Mr J. P. Morier, the
British charge d'affaires, reported that a set of American desperadoes, posing as a convention of Spanish
subjects, had seized Baton Rouge and declared the
province independent. A month later, the rumour was
current that the United States had agreed with the
convention to despatch a Governor. A Committee of
the Senate had reported that, " If we look forward to
the free use of the Mississippi, the Mobile, and the
Apalachicola, and the other rivers of the West, by ourselves and our posterity, New Orleans and the Floridas
must become a part of the United States, either by
purchase or by conquest." The presidential message,
therefore, announced the occupation of West Florida
so far as it was claimed by the United States, not
as an act of war, but pending the discussion of the
question. Morier, unable to galvanise Spain into pre-
cautions, or to extort from the Secretary of State
anything more than a promise of explanations in
London, vented his indignation in a bitter description
to his Government of the Congressional Debates from
December 18th onwards. " These immaculate republicans," he reported, " conscious of the weakness of their
case, very quietly reconcile the usurpation to their
conscience on the pretence of self-defence." Both
Houses had gone into secret Session, and showed the
national appreciation of the crisis by debating many
days with closed doors. When, towards the end of
June, a newspaper tore down the veil, it was seen that

just one month before Monroe took office as Secretary of State, the Doctrine which bears his name had been in part outlined by Madison and accepted by the Houses. In a confidential message recommending to Congress the policy of taking temporary possession of West Florida, the President had advised " A declaration that the United States could not see, without serious inquietude, any part of a neighbouring territory in which they have, in different respects, so deep and just a concern, pass from the hands of Spain into those of any other foreign power." A long and secret debate had followed, and on the evening of Sunday, March 3rd, Congress had passed a resolution, or declaration, accepting the policy of the President. " Taking into view the peculiar situation of Spain," they said, " and of her American Provinces, and considering the influence which the destiny of the territory adjoining the southern boundary of the United States may have upon their security, tranquillity, and commerce...the United States, under the peculiar circumstances of the existing crisis, cannot, without serious inquietude, see any part of the said territory pass into the hands of any other foreign power." Having thus placed on record their motives, Congress proceeded to pass an act for the occupation of West Florida.

This Madison Doctrine, as amended by Congress, seems in part to surpass and in part to fall short of the language of 1823. It is more fortunate than the Monroe Doctrine in receiving the sanction of the Legislature, and it is at once translated into action. It is, on the other hand, a particular solution, not a general principle, and instead of dictating to the world

the permanent inviolability of a hemisphere, it almost
apologetically provides for the momentary safety of the
United States. What is common to both declarations
is the assumption by the United States of a right to
limit the action of foreign powers with regard to
territory within the western hemisphere but beyond
their own borders, in order to prevent possible injury
to their own interests ; and the treatment of theories
of destiny as a factor in international relations.

Destiny, in the days of Madison, however, revealed
herself in far less shadowy guise than that in which
she had appeared to the statesmen of the Revolution.
Washington had founded the Union, and had be-
queathed to it a policy which above all things may
be called American. Jefferson, repeating his precepts,
had doubled the area to which they might apply. And
now Madison, though Spain brands his conduct as
'treacherous,' and England laughs at its pretence of
righteousness, receives the tribute of an enemy to the
advance of the Republic. In a despatch so biting that
the hand of authority at home has removed the possibility of international offence by blotting out several
lines, Morier jeers at the lack of energy to be expected
from a State with an army of five thousand men and
an empty treasury. He is compelled to acknowledge,
however, that "The Floridas, from their situation and
from the rapid increase of population in this country"
are " destined to form a part of the government of the
United States." Ten years later, when Monroe had
become President and the number of United States
had risen to twenty-four, this destiny received its
fulfilment. The Floridas, burdensome to Spain, were

in 1819 assigned by treaty to the Republic; and in 1821, after a thousand perils, the treaty received the ratification of King Ferdinand.

The scale of political power in North America thus turned decisively in favour of the United States. Their increasing importance was attested by their relations with foreign powers. In deference rather to internal faction than to Spain, they renounced the unsubstantial claim to Texas, but Great Britain shrank from opposing their preparations to make settlements within the area drained by the Columbia River—a territory which she regarded as her own. While their northern neighbour showed herself thus little disposed to resist them, the provinces on their south-western frontier passed from the sway of Spain to a state of precarious and un-aggressive independence. Thus potent in their own continent, therefore, the United States gained credit with the world outside. Cuba, the Ionian Islands, and even Greece, were ready to welcome their interference. Humoured, if not feared, by Great Britain, courted by Spain, by France, by the Holy Alliance, and by the South Americans, with unity at home and a generation of unprecedented progress to look back upon, their faith in their destiny increased, and the Monroe Doctrine expressed it.

CHAPTER II.

THE INTERNATIONAL SITUATION IN 1823.

ALTHOUGH an augmented territory and, still more, a swelling spirit of self-confidence were required before Americans could utter the words of 1823, it must not be supposed that the Monroe Doctrine was called forth by internal considerations alone. It must rather be regarded as the product of complex circumstances existing in America, North and South, and in Europe. To investigate its origin, then, we must define the national factors which were at work, and examine the contact between them by which the result in question was produced. The United States, indeed, gave the Doctrine birth, but writers and statesmen have often ascribed its paternity to Great Britain. The former opposed it chiefly to the Holy Alliance; the latter, it is probable, to France. Spain and Spanish America were the parties to the quarrel which it was designed to bring to a close.

The attitude and motives of Great Britain admit of brief statement. Two great principles seem to have governed all her action after the downfall of Napoleon. Her newly-won commercial supremacy must be maintained and developed, and the slave-trade must be

swept from the face of the earth. Thus far public
opinion was supreme, but in other directions the
Ministry was unchecked by popular feeling.

Having shared in the salvation of Europe, and in
the arbitrary settlement of her destinies at Vienna,
Great Britain did not at once cease to exercise that
guardianship and supervision of the Continent with
which a common danger had invested the Allies.
Wellington and Castlereagh felt no repugnance at
the principles of Metternich or the aspirations of
Alexander. While not desirous of meddling in the
government of Russia, Austria and Prussia, as being
" branches of one Christian nation," and while resolved
not to tolerate any extension of such government to
their own country, a king and ministers in daily
danger from mobs and assassins could hardly fail to
sympathise with the Holy Alliance as upholding
authority against revolution. Between constitutional
and autocratic government, however, there could be
no lasting union, and in May 1820 a British State
paper laid down in the clearest terms the principle
of national independence. This principle, however,
was not fully maintained, and British sanction of the
government of Europe by Congresses not finally withdrawn, until in September 1822 George Canning was
placed by Liverpool in the office left vacant by the
death of Castlereagh. The policy of the new Foreign
Secretary, though not bellicose, was essentially British.
Pursuing her own ends in her own way, striving to
hold the balance between the contending principles
of absolutism and democracy, Great Britain recovered
her independence and her isolation. Still a member of

the Quintuple Alliance, and influential at the Court of Vienna, she escaped the violent hostility of Europe, but retained the real friendship only of weaklings such as Sweden and Portugal. Canning's system of policy, indeed, if his secretary understood it aright, was opportunistic and mechanical. The interests of Great Britain were to be regarded as a plane, which, if depressed in any part, must be restored to its general level by elevation elsewhere. In carrying out this system, he endeavoured by favouring revolution in Spanish America to counterbalance the success of legitimacy in Spain, where the French armies had restored despotic government. To further the plan he called for the help of the United States; and the negotiations for this help, though not directly successful, determined the time and manner of the enunciation of the Monroe Doctrine.

In seeking the help of the United States Canning was but little handicapped by history. After the miserable and indecisive war of 1812—14, Great Britain had shown herself nervously anxious to avoid all chance of further rupture. Actual concessions were made most grudgingly, but the discussion of disputed points was, whenever possible, postponed, and Castlereagh allowed English Ministers at Washington to be active only on the subject of the slave-trade. The result was that the American people might regard the British nation as afraid to provoke the victors of New Orleans, while their Secretary of State wrote down her policy as " wavering and unsteady,"—" willing to wound and yet afraid to strike." Canning, however, upheld the system of conciliation, and in 1823 something like concert between the two governments had been arrived at.

In that year the interests of both were threatened by the conduct of France and of the Holy Alliance. The story of the relations between France and the United States forms a curious chapter in the history of sentimental alliances between nations. The frenzy of enthusiasm for American liberty that had driven Lafayette across the ocean while fashionable Paris thronged round Franklin, had calmed as quickly as it had risen. In the negotiations at Versailles, France was not altogether on the side of her protege, while the American Commissioners showed a want of gratitude and good faith in signing preliminaries of peace without consulting her. Among the people of the United States, however, the Republican or Democratic party, claiming the allegiance of Jefferson, Madison and Monroe, was in its origin the disciple and devotee of France. The outbreak of the Revolution, therefore, was the signal for the frantic approbation of America; and Monroe, her ambassador at Paris, showed that he fully shared in it. We can hardly understand the rapture, indeed, which must have filled young America at the sight of a mighty European nation determining to tread with them the untried path of Republicanism. Four million people, it must never be forgotten, were putting to the proof a form of government of which the Christian era had seen no real example, while the monarchs of the Old World frowned and prophesied evils to come. It is the proudest trophy of their government that at such a moment the pen of Jefferson could formulate against France broad principles of neutrality to which time has added nothing. Washington must have had the Democrats and France in view when in his famous Farewell Address he solemnly warned the American people against "the insidious wiles of foreign influence......one of the most baneful foes of republican government," dooming the small or weak nation to be the satellite of its great and powerful favourite.

One year later, France and the United States found themselves at war. The overbearing government of the Directory had dictated humiliation and corruption as the attitude of the Americans, and Pinckney had immortalised himself by the reply "Millions for defense, but not a cent for tribute." John Adams, the Federal President, showed true but unpopular patriotism by nipping the war in the bud, and in September, 1800, a Convention was concluded. With the new century, the democratic party triumphed; and, up to the promulgation of the Monroe Doctrine, the harmony between the two nations was never seriously impaired. Napoleon, having acquired Louisiana from Spain, did not hesitate to shock the feelings of his ally by selling it to the United States; and Jefferson, President from 1800 to 1809, so far forgot his Democratic principles as to strengthen the Federal bond by purchasing it as a national possession. So long as the First Empire continued, however, there can be little doubt that the Republican institutions of America were exposed to danger from France, while in England even George III had accepted as irrevocable the verdict of 1783. Sentiment and tradition, however, proved too strong for political wisdom. When, in the struggle between the rivals, the rights of the United States were invaded by both alike, hereditary sympathy for France caused the government of Madison to choose Great Britain for its foe.

The events of 1815 left France a monarchy, England pledged to its preservation, and the United States at peace with both. In the New World, Louis XVIII had few apparent interests. The ambition of his ministers, however, caused the United States some uneasiness, in particular lest Cuba might be ceded to France by Spain. Montmorency, as Minister for Foreign Affairs, had despatched secret agents to America, and Chateaubriand, his successor, followed the same policy, in the hope of transforming the insurgent republics into monarchies under Bourbon sovereigns. The danger first seemed imminent, however, when France, having stationed an army of observation to prevent yellow fever and constitutional principles from crossing her southern frontier, gained the goodwill of the allied sovereigns in a design for putting down the Spanish revolution. She succeeded in the task, and nothing seemed to the administration at Washington more likely than that, monarchical principles apart, she should indemnify herself by wresting from Spain its claims to some of the revolted colonies. Canning, at the same time, saw the tacit revival of the Bourbon Family Compact. The Pyrenees had fallen, but he was resolved to maintain the Atlantic Ocean. In the interests of England and of Europe he sought the aid of the United States, at the moment when their fears had been raised on account of America. Prince Polignac, the French Ambassador in London, it was true, disclaimed for his country any aims at trans-atlantic conquest. Even had the news of this dis-claimer reached the Monroe Cabinet, however, it could not have blinded them to the fact that the French Ministers were neither omnipotent nor unanimous. The presidential message of 1823, in so far as it warned France to go no farther, was a boon to the Old World devised in the interests of the New.

Though the peril from the power actually under arms was perhaps more real, greater danger of an extension to the New World of the political system of the Old seemed to the United States to come from the Holy Alliance. This league of European sovereigns under the hegemony of the Czar, though less capable than France of determining a policy, seemed infinitely more capable of putting it into execution. Originally conceived of by Alexander, perhaps, as a society for the realisation of Christian principles of government, it had degenerated into an association of autocrats to stifle every aspiration after constitutional freedom. Of this association, to which the sovereigns of Russia, Austria, Prussia, France, Spain, Naples and Sardinia had fully pledged themselves, the Austrian Chancellor, Metternich, was the centre and the soul. Castlereagh he had esteemed his second self—devoted to him in heart and spirit. Canning he was bound to regard with more distrust, but he clung to the hope that England might be induced to continue that policy of general acquiescence in the acts of the Holy Alliance which she had not yet finally abjured.

The United States, on the other hand, had repulsed the persistent overtures of the Czar to accede to the

Holy Alliance.   Their government had come to regard it as "a mere hypocritical fraud," while they knew that Alexander and Metternich regarded the Republic as "a standing refutation of their doctrines."   When it is added that Monroe and his advisers believed both that Great Britain might be induced to return to her allegiance, and that the object of the European league was the overthrow of liberty, first in South and then in North America, the relation of the Holy Alliance to the words of 1823 becomes clearer.

The danger to America from the Holy Alliance, or from France, or from both powers seemed to be made imminent by the events of 1823 in the Peninsula.

The intervention of France in Spain, opposed by Canning in Paris, London, and Madrid with an eloquence lacking nothing but success, was sanctioned, though not dictated, by the Holy Allies.   The revolutionary Ministers and Cortes, although their government had estranged the mass of the nation, held it a point of honour to present an unyielding front to the French demands ; and on the 6th April the Duc d'Angouleme crossed the Bidassoa.   The slightness of the resistance offered to her troops almost lent colour to the professions of France that she was not at war with her neighbour.   The Cortes carried the king to Seville, and before the close of May D'Angouleme had entered Madrid.   He had now only to obtain the release of Ferdinand, who was dragged by the Cortes to Cadiz, and there besieged.   In the last extremity, the Constitutionalists decided to throw themselves on the mercy of their king, and on the 1st October they allowed him to join the French army.

2—2

The fall of Cadiz seemed an ill omen for the liberties of America. Ferdinand abandoned himself to a reactionary Reign of Terror, which D'Angouleme was unable to check. Order could be maintained only by the troops of France, and it was vain to look to the shattered finances of Spain for their support. France, though Chateaubriand was anything but mercenary, might seek indemnity in the New World; and the state of the young republics promised her little difficulty in finding it. As the informal agent of the Holy Alliance, therefore, she had brought about a state of things in Spain which revived European interest in Spanish America. So long as the mother-country had been tainted with constitutional principles, the cause of absolutism could gain little from a crusade to restore her rule. When the clerical party was clamouring for the Inquisition, however, no one could doubt that the doctrines of Legitimacy would be sufficiently maintained. In Naples, in Piedmont and in Spain, interference had triumphed. Was it not due to themselves, to Ferdinand and to the world, that the Allies should turn to America—to bring rebels under the sceptre of their sovereign, and to check the contagion of example?

Such was, in brief, the position of the United States, Great Britain, France, the Holy Alliance and Spain in the international situation out of which the Monroe Doctrine arose. To describe this situation is to become conscious of an influence which, though vague, was felt on all sides—the influence of Spanish America.

The huge empire founded in the sixteenth century

by Cortes and Pizarro had for three hundred years remained almost without a history. Within a frontier of many thousand miles, Spain had decreed death to the foreigner who should set foot in her possessions. In the memory of the generation which achieved the independence of Columbia, the rule had been broken only by three Frenchmen and a Danish doctor. Natives who on any pretext traded with the foreigner, were pitilessly condemned to death. When, during the Peninsular War, some of the Spanish colonies in South America were impelled by the vicissitudes of the home government to act for themselves, their population, resources and aspirations were unknown outside their borders. When the eyes of North Americans had been fixed on them for fifteen years, and Monroe had officially championed their cause, few, it was held indisputable, could discern clearly their actual condition. Even at the present day, their share in the events which preceded the Monroe Doctrine has received but little attention.

In the appendix to this essay an attempt is made, with the help of contemporary evidence, to describe Spanish America at the time of the Monroe Doctrine.

The policy pursued by Great Britain with regard to the revolted colonies during the period anterior to the Monroe Doctrine seems to have been opportunistic. The forces impelling her to action long rested in equilibrium. In South, as in North America, British commerce was the lode-star of the British statesman. Regarding the ancient colonial exclusion as suspended if not abrogated by events, he taught Spain to enter into a "tacit compact" to countenance the British trader, at least while the struggle continued. This gained, it was easiest to let events take their own course. A treaty of neutrality was conceded to Spain, and to enforce it Parliament imitated the legislation of the United States against Foreign Enlistment. Offers of mediation were made in 1810, 1812, and 1815, but without result. Their failure was attributed by Canning to the obstinacy of the Spanish government, but by hostile critics to the captiousness and insincerity of Great Britain. On the one hand, Spain had for years been the ward of England, and her guardian could not be indifferent to the ruin of her empire and finances. More than one half of Liverpool's colleagues, again, were ultra-Tories, and all would in the abstract regret to see monarchical institutions displaced by republican. The prevailing ignorance of the spirit, resources and dispositions of the South Americans was an additional deterrent from action. Until time gave them the lie, the friends of Ferdinand and Metternich never wearied of repeating that the rebels might overthrow, but could never construct a government. On the other hand, the Spanish colonial system was acknowledged by all Europe to be an anachronism, and even Spain could not deny that the exercise of her power over some of the colonies was interrupted. The United States pressed Great Britain to take the lead in acknowledging the independence of the provinces which had evidently terminated in their own favour the contest with the mother-country. The cry was echoed by the agents of the provinces themselves, and by a growing chorus of British subjects with South American interests. If the preferences of the new

States were disregarded, the restoration of a modified
form of Spanish government seemed the most con-
venient solution of the difficulty; and all parties
joined in beseeching Spain to take steps to terminate
the anarchy and to strive to end the contest on such
terms as these. Their appeal, however, save when the
government of Spain was constitutional, and therefore
offensive to the Holy Alliance, fell on deaf ears.
Spain denied much, hoped much, and did nothing.
Meanwhile the forces striving to overcome the inertia
of Great Britain slowly gathered strength. By a
regular series of steps, she was driven to warn Spain,
to threaten her, to seek independent information as to
the new States, and to declare to the Court of Madrid
that her action with regard to them would be likewise
independent. To the final display of this independence,
she was spurred by the United States, which first
recognised the new Republics, and then, by promul-
gating the Monroe Doctrine, seemed to come forth as
their protector.

Opposition to the interference of Europe in South
America had thus for some time engaged the attention
of Great Britain. Her policy with regard to the new
states had, as we have seen, aimed chiefly at promoting
her commerce. Its success is attested by the fact that,
at the end of 1823, even the Prime Minister of France
spoke of her as the power most immediately interested in the affairs of South America. According to
Chateaubriand himself, the new republics had become
a species of English colonies. As her stake increased,
however, she more and more felt the need of gaining
for it the protection of a government. Her own

political prepossessions, as Canning confessed, were in favour of monarchy, and even of the restoration of a modified Spanish rule. Her commissioners to the new States, therefore, were instructed to promote, though not to propose, a settlement in accordance with these principles; and the Russian Ambassador at Madrid believed that they might save Mexico from Republicanism. The success of the Colonies and the obstinacy of Spain had justified her, none the less, in asserting full liberty of action, and the British commercial classes began to exercise a steady pressure on their Government. In 1822, the merchants and shipowners of Liverpool and the merchants and manufacturers of Glasgow impressed upon Canning their desire for the establishment of political relations between Great Britain and South America. Next year, the request for consuls and protection was renewed by the Chambers of Commerce of Manchester and Belfast, by the Shipowners' Society, and by numerous British merchants. Canning, meanwhile, had been seeking the assistance of the Board of Trade, the Treasury, and the King's Advocate, and in the middle of October he was able to announce that consuls would be sent forthwith to twelve places in Spanish America. Formal recognition of the new governments, on the other hand, would offend Spain and the Allies without clearly benefiting Great Britain. Canning disclaimed the quest of exclusive commercial advantages, and the new states had nothing else save their gratitude to offer. He was resolved, moreover, that Spain should have no ground on which to impugn the good faith of British neutrality, and up to the present she had denied the facts on which alone impartial recognition could be founded. He was content, therefore, to secure protection for commerce, and despatched commissioners to examine South America, as a preliminary to proceeding further. The policy of Spain towards Spanish America, then, was dictated by pride; that of Great Britain, by interest. In September, 1823, indeed, Canning had informed Polignac that, whenever the position of Spain should be hopeless, " neither justice, nor humanity, nor the interests either of Europe or of America, would, in the opinion of His Majesty's Government, allow that the struggle...should be taken up afresh by other hands;" but would rather prescribe recognition. This, however, is almost the sole allusion by an European Power to any interest that the Americans might possess in their own destiny. As mere belligerents, it is true, they could claim no strict *right* to be treated as adult states. But so soon as it was evident that they possessed all the distinctive features of a sovereign power,—the absence of foreign control, a definite territory, and, above all, a civilised government desirous of entering the family of nations,—they acquired at least a moral title to consideration ; and to facts and morals alike Europe seemed to have shut her eyes. Great Britain, the power best informed and most concerned, could not join the rest in pleading that the principle of legitimacy stood in the way. The United States, on the other hand, seemed to have pursued a more disinterested policy. They had in fact exposed themselves to the charge of being too hasty in recognizing some of the new communities. It is significant that while Great Britain sent consuls,—the sure proof of local interest,—

before diplomatists, the United States sometimes reversed the order. Long solicited by agents from South America, the government at Washington sent commissioners thither in 1818. Several of the men chosen were known to be fanatics in the cause of emancipation, and in their reports their political opinions were faithfully reproduced. In 1822, however, the Government, spurred on by Henry Clay, took the decisive step, and recognized Columbia, Mexico, Buenos Ayres, Chili and Peru as sovereign and independent states. It is possible to hold the view that in this measure the United States exceeded their duty in order to steal a march on Great Britain. The evidence shows, however, that many of their people genuinely sympathised with the South Americans. Their enthusiasm rose as they saw how the revolutions externally resembled their own. Bolivar was acclaimed as a second—even a greater—Washington, and the fetters of the old Foreign Enlistment Act were too weak to prevent them from helping him. Their feelings were shared by some at least of the administration. The Secretary of State, indeed, laughed at those who stood "looking in ecstatic gaze at South America, foretelling liberty to it as the Jews foretell the Messiah ;" but his words show that only a bold man would declare that he saw with other eyes. The President had for years declared in his messages the sympathy of the people of the North with their Southern brethren. The Secretary of the Treasury had in 1817 advocated a mission of enquiry into their position, and next year the Cabinet had discussed the question "whether an armed force should be sent to visit both sides of the coast of South

America, for the protection of our commerce, and to countenance the patriots." They formally invited Great Britain and France to join in recognizing Buenos Ayres, the independence of which appeared to be established. The British Government left such sympathy to Mackintosh and the opposition.

CHAPTER III.

JAMES MONROE AND HIS CABINET.

SUCH then, was the position and policy of the national factors in the production of the Monroe Doctrine. The Doctrine itself, however, was formulated by Americans to promote American interests. It is to the United States, therefore, that we must look for a continuous history of its evolution. Great Britain, France, the Holy Alliance, Spain and Spanish America all helped to shape it, but they could guide the hand of Monroe only through their influence upon his constituents. This influence can usually first be appreciated in the Cabinet—a body of some six heads of the departments of state nominated and consulted by the President. The spheres of the Legislature and Executive, indeed, can in no Government be wholly separate. The administration of the United States could complete none of the greater acts of foreign policy without the assent of the Senate to a treaty or of the House to an appropriation. The Monroe Cabinet knew this, and their Democratic principles forbade them to strive against it. The result, the outcome of political prudence, was that before leading they looked to see whether the representatives of the people would follow. The Legislature viewed askance the project of annexing the Floridas, and the Executive, which desired the annexation, recommended its postponement. The Legislature showed its sympathy with the South Americans, and the Executive, with a clear conscience, discovered that the time had come at which the United States would do well to grant them recognition. The several members of the Executive, again, though they still scorned to court the favour of the electorate, could not forget that their own position was but temporary. Human nature forbade them to watch passively their political rivals captivating the Assemblies from which they themselves were excluded. Their ambition and their circumstances alike impelled them towards a popular policy. The Presidential message was their annual manifesto to the country, and the instructions to diplomatists abroad the side on which the Constitution trammelled them the least.

The principles of the Cabinet of Monroe are deducible from eight years' practice. From 1817 to 1825 the same hands held the reins, and at the close of that time the President was able with satisfaction to review his administration as a whole. Foreign affairs had been controlled without interruption by John Quincy Adams, but never without the supervision of Monroe, himself promoted from the office of Secretary of State. What Adams and Monroe devised, J. C. Calhoun, the Secretary for War, and at times William Wirt, the Attorney-General, had criticised. The Secretary of the Treasury, W. H. Crawford, when not incapacitated by ill-health, had shown himself a bitter rival of Adams. A few officials of less weight had at times shared in the deliberations; and from outside the Cabinet had received impulses from two men of striking character—Andrew Jackson and Henry Clay. The former, by his military severity in the South, did much to influence their relations with Spain, and, not impossibly, with Mexico; while the latter, glowing in the cause of universal liberty, harassed ministers by his ascendancy in the House of Representatives.

In Monroe and Adams, the United States had secured strong and honest men to fill the chief places of its government. United, they could dominate the Cabinet, and when their opinions on foreign affairs coincide, it would be idle to look further for the source of its policy. For eight years, indeed, harmony prevailed between them. Their political opinions, none the less, differed widely; while in personality few men could be more unlike. Monroe, a Virginian, and a descendant of the Cavaliers, was old enough to have won renown in the War of Independence, and to have sat in the Continental Congress which followed it. An uncompromising democrat, he opposed the Constitution, but sat in the Senate until despatched on an adventurous embassy to the government of the Directory. His enthusiasm for France, however, carried him too far for the approbation of his Government, and in two years he was superseded and recalled. His rejoinder was a lengthy indictment of the Executive, which evoked the strong and detailed censure of Washington. Virginia, none the less, made him her Governor, and maintained him in office till 1803, when he was again dispatched to Europe. He reached Paris in time to share with Livingston the honour of arranging for the purchase of Louisiana. Negotiations with Great Britain and Spain, however, brought him only political experience, and on his return to America, he again defended himself with his pen. Virginia, though preferring Madison for President, once more elected him Governor, and in 1811, immediately after the seizure of West Florida, he became Secretary of State. In this capacity, his utmost efforts were called forth by the struggle with England, of which he has been called "the prime mover." Summoned to the War Department by the failure of the first three campaigns, he checked the British triumph with unflinching determination till peace was signed. Thenceforward the lustre of his career was less dimmed by failure. In 1817, he was chosen to succeed Madison by so overwhelming a majority that he could afford to regard the Federalist Party as extinguished. He was happy in possessing ability sufficient for his post without being so great as to arouse jealousy. In the reception of foreigners his awkwardness and lack of fluency were concealed by the dignified reserve which he believed that his office demanded, while in intercourse with Americans such defects were obliterated by his kindness and courtesy to all. Experience had developed in him a leniency of judgment and a magnanimity that did much to make him beloved. Though at times he might seem impressionable and stubborn, he was fitted to lead a cabinet by his readiness to receive advice and by his firmness when he had once made up his mind. Above all, he was entirely and inflexibly honest. His soul, men felt, "might be turned wrong side outwards without discovering a blemish to the world." From his own character, as much as from the paucity of burning questions, his Presidency was called "the era of good feeling," and the chorus of his praise was marred by scarcely one discordant note. His opponents could only declare that his career was closed, and that he had not the slightest influence in Congress. Jefferson and Madison were among his oldest and most faithful friends, and he could reprove Andrew Jackson without causing a cloud to rise between them. His chief eulogist was, after his death, his ambitious lieutenant, the harsh and outspoken J. Q. Adams. Better than formal panegyric is the narrative, mingled as it is with criticism, in which the Secretary of State has recorded his daily intercourse with the President. Other subordinates took no less warm a tone. "A noble-minded man he was," says Richard Rush, "without a particle of selfishness or ill-directed ambition in his whole nature; a man of Roman mould; honest, fearless and magnanimous." "Love of country and devotion to duty" appeared to one who knew him intimately to be the causes of his position and repute. "There was not the least particle of conceit in Mr Monroe, and yet he seemed always strongly to feel that he had rendered great public service...He was wholly unselfish." Viewed with English eyes, he appears in no darker colours. Early in the century, Lord Holland found him "plain in his manners, and somewhat slow in his apprehension, but...diligent, earnest, sensible and even profound." During his Presidency, he impressed Stratford Canning, no friendly critic of Americans, as "really an amiable and upright man," whose personal character diminished the risks of fresh quarrel between Great Britain and the United States. In a word, he is portrayed throughout his life as sound, but never as brilliant, firm to execute, but unlikely to originate.

In almost every point save that of honesty, J. Q. Adams was the antithesis of Monroe. A new Englander and Puritan, the son of the second President of the United States, he had begun his career as a member of that Federalist party which his father had led to its destruction. Monroe had been educated on the battle-field; Adams, in the embassy. A scholar almost from his birth, he found life without Cicero and Tacitus like "a privation of one of his limbs." His ability was great, and his ambition equalled it. His self-confidence could not fail to be increased by the strength which enabled him in middle life to battle for an hour with the current of the Potomac, and to toil with unremitting diligence in a climate which surrounded him with "vermin of all filths." A fluent speaker, he lamented that in social intercourse he was "by nature a silent animal." His "coarseness and violence" evoked the bitter complaints of the young Stratford Canning, and nearly sixty years later, his "very uneven temper" and "manner somewhat too often domineering" were not forgotten. From his childhood as a diplomat to his old age as an obstructionist congressman, he was above all things original. His invaluable Diary, as well as the witness of his contemporaries, shows that in affairs of private and public life alike he thought out his prin-ciples and acted upon them, without the slightest regard for the opinions and feelings of others. His judgments, even of himself, show a prevailing tendency to harshness. In the midst of the most violent explosions of wrath, his head was cool and his vision clear; but he never learned to tolerate men whose opinions differed from his own. Matchless in ability, diligence and uprightness, he commanded respect rather than love. As President, his administration was never popular. Monroe had been re-elected by a practically unanimous vote. Adams, chosen in the first instance almost by accident, was defeated in 1829 by Andrew Jackson.

Under the guidance of Monroe and Adams the foreign policy of the Administration was a policy of peace and patriotism. In securing peace, their best friend was the Atlantic Ocean. Despatches from England to Washington breathe little of the air of mutual suspicion and intrigue that seems vital to the capitals of Europe. The Minister of the United States in London can congratulate himself that for his country he has only to be just and fear not. At several courts the Republic was not yet represented, and everywhere its agents were notorious for their lack of secrecy. The attitude of the powers of Europe towards the United States, again, was designed to express friendship. Great Britain, with whom alone there was chronic danger of a rupture, showed herself nervously anxious for peace. Her representatives in the United States were instructed above all things to be conciliatory. Two years after the Treaty of Ghent, the lawless execution of two British subjects by Andrew Jackson in Florida roused the nation, but the Ministry refused to hold up the finger which would have let slip the dogs of war. The subjects in dispute between the two countries were submitted to a general negotiation; and a convention in respect to the north-western territorial dispute, of a merely temporising character was the result. Though the British press was indignant at the cession of the Floridas, ministers forbore to frown upon it, and disclaimed all share in causing Spain to delay its ratification. Castlereagh, indeed, was regarded by the United States as their friend, and when he was succeeded by "the dashing and flashy spirit of George Canning," something like sympathy between the two Governments had been established.

Individual monarchs of the Holy Alliance vied for the favour of the trans-Atlantic republicans. The Spanish Minister desired their alliance, and his French colleague concluded a commercial convention with them. Austria hinted a wish to exchange diplomatists, and Portugal laid before them a scheme for the Federation of the New World. With Russia, extraordinary amity prevailed. The Czar had consented to overlook the violation of Legitimacy involved in the very existence of the United States so far as to propose that they should join the Holy Alliance. Monroe had reciprocated his friendliness by forgiving his minister for behaviour which from the representative of Great Britain would have hazarded war. Alexander himself was entrusted with the arbitration of disputes arising out of the Treaty of Ghent, and when his Ukase was held to invade the rights and even the territory of the United States, the diplomatic calm remained unruffled. The policy of peace, it was clear, would be broken only in a cause exclusively American. The fate of Florida, of Cuba, and finally of Spanish America became in turn the burning question of the day. For none of them, indeed, were the people really anxious to fight. It is to the credit of the President and Cabinet, none the less, that they avoided extraneous sources of war. The Holy Alliance courted them in vain. Refusing to acknowledge that the United States could have more than a commercial interest in the Mediterranean, they declined to acquire the Ionian Islands. In spite of the strongly-worded sympathy of the Presidential Message, they rejected the prayer of the Greeks for "recognition, alliance and assistance." They waited nearly two years, though with an ill grace, for Spain to ratify the cession of Florida; and they refused to receive Cuba at the price of assisting her to throw off the Spanish yoke. They seem even to have refrained from encouraging Guatemala to cede its territory to the Union as the price of protection for its people.

Their policy, then, was patriotic in that they pursued the real advantage of their own country by avoiding entanglements with foreign powers. Where its interests were really concerned, however, they showed no lack of firmness. Inspired by the President, they carried out a scheme of national defence. An island claimed by Spain had become a nest of pirates. and they did not hesitate to occupy it. On the same principle, they showed a disposition to interfere in Texas, though as yet without the design of annexation. Ancient claims against Spain had been vindicated by a law professing to establish a kind of United States mortgage on the territory of Florida, and they informed South American belligerents that no third power could be allowed to prejudice the rights thereby acquired. They commissioned Andrew Jackson, if the need arose, to pursue hostile Indians into Spanish territory, and the commission was carried out. On the ground that they could not subject citizens of the United States to the judgment of foreigners, they rejected the slave-trade convention for which Great Britain was clamouring. In the far north-west, they allowed no British claim to check the development of the Republic. In their South American policy, again, though defying the Holy Alliance, they declined "to come in as a cock-boat in the wake of the British man-of-war." They took the lead in recognising the new states, and they crowned the work by enunciating the Monroe Doctrine.

This policy of peace and patriotism, of confining themselves to America and brooking no interference within their sphere, Monroe and his Cabinet were not unwilling to defend on grounds of principle. Though fully aware of the repugnance of Europe to republicanism, the President seized every opportunity of proclaiming his belief in that "most excellent system of government." He strove with tongue and pen to show that the United States system would soon attain to what Burke and Wellington claimed for the British—"the highest degree of perfection of which human institutions are capable." His public utterances, moreover, rivalled those of Clay and the House of Representatives in their expressions of sympathy with the peoples in the Old World and in the New who were struggling to free themselves from absolute monarchy. Adams also, though he objected to such paragraphs as exotics in the presidential Messages, did not hesitate to express to the British Minister his own opinions on European

politics.   Early in 1823, he commented with severity
on the principles expressed by France, and stated his
satisfaction at the policy of Great Britain, "more particularly as it affected the great principle of national
independence, which he seemed to consider as brought
into immediate danger by what he termed, the im-
pending conflict ʻbetween autocracy and parliamentary
government ʼ."   " The whole system of colonisation," he
had previously maintained, "was an abuse of government, and it was time that it should come to an end."
Speaking as a private individual, he is said to have
argued that Great Britain had no *right* to prevent her
colonies from being supplied by the United States;
while in a Fourth of July oration he voiced the
sentiments of the people by a ferocious attack on the
American policy of George the Third.

Expressions of opinion such as these, however,
might be defended as domestic.   The Secretary of
State, at least, was anxious to go further.   In declaring
his determination to refuse to receive ministers from
South America, the Czar had enunciated to the United
States the principles of the Holy Alliance.   At the
same time the constitutional cause in Spain was totter-
ing to its fall, and Great Britain was making overtures
to the United States which they desired to decline.
Adams declared the time ripe for the Administration to
proclaim republican principles to the world, and at the
first blush "this idea was acquiesced in on all sides."
Later councils, it is true, suggested doubts and difficulties, and the scheme was in part withdrawn.   There
can be little doubt, however, as will be shown hereafter,
that it was embodied in the message of the President,

and that the patriotic policy of the Cabinet found its expression in the Monroe Doctrine.

The policy of peace and patriotism may be further illustrated from the annals of the years during which it prevailed. One of the earliest acts of the Monroe Administration was the dispatch of three citizens to examine the condition of South America. Next year, neither the troubles in Florida nor the disagreement of the commissioners prevented the South American question from making substantial progress. Rush and Castlereagh mutually disclaimed the pursuit of exclusive advantages in commerce, and the United States had decided to stand aloof from the mediation between Spain and her colonies which the congress of Aix-la-Chapelle proposed. Spurred on by Clay, however, at the end of the year they requested the co-operation of Great Britain and France in the recognition of Buenos Ayres. Though the allies had failed to devise a plan of mediation. the answer of both was unfavourable, and for the time being Buenos Ayres was obscured by Florida. In the spring of 1819, Spain offered to satisfy the claims of the United States against her by ceding the province to them in full sovereignty, and her plenipotentiary signed a treaty to this effect. On grounds which seemed insufficient, however, the Court of Madrid withheld its ratification, and for two years the Administration of the United States wavered between diplomacy and force. Their suspicions pointed to Great Britain as the cause of delay, but Castlereagh showed that he had given instructions with an opposite tendency. Russia lent her influence at Madrid, and France sent word that the great stumblingblock was the policy of the United States towards South America. A Commission, however, had been sent to Brazil, and the general cause of recognition was upheld by resolutions of the House of Representatives carried by the influence of Clay. The South American envoys, especially those from Columbia, clamoured for favours in the supply of arms, and their northern champions complained of the restrictions of the Act restraining Foreign Enlistment. The embarrassments of the Administration were completed by anxiety with regard to Cuba, while in the autumn of 1820 Stratford Canning arrived with instructions to press home the subject of the slave-trade. The triumph of the Constitutionalists in Spain, however, brought relief. It cooled the feelings of the Holy Alliance with regard to Spanish America, and it facilitated the ratification of the treaty ceding the Floridas. In 1821, therefore, the President could enter on his second term of office with an Address of general congratulation. The events of the year, however, were hardly calculated to bear him out. The violence of Andrew Jackson as Governor of Florida roused the wrath of Spain, while the discussion with reference to settlements at the mouth of the Columbia River alienated the minister of Great Britain. At the same time, Clay was urging the House of Representatives to force the hand of the Executive with regard to South America, and every question was liable to complication by the struggle for the Presidency. The year closed with the reception of the Russian Ukase, by which Alexander claimed the coast of North America as far as the 51st parallel of latitude, and denounced confiscation against the ship and cargo which should approach within 100 Italian miles of the shore. The foreign policy of 1822 was marked by the recognition of South America, dictated by a special presidential message in March. The Spanish Minister protested in vain, and the necessary measures were carried with little excitement or debate. In June, a *charge d'affaires* from Columbia was formally received at Washington, and early next year, the President determined to send diplomatic agents to all the more important Spanish American States. The recognition, however, was felt by many to be premature. As in their own revolution, so now in favouring the revolution of their imitators, the United States were conscious of their isolation. In the interests of liberty and of their republic, therefore, it became their object to induce other powers to follow them, and the power to which they turned was Great Britain. With regard to the north-west coast, the Administration, though treating the question as of no great moment, never dreamed of submission to the pretensions set up by Russia. They took steps to develop commerce with France and England, and in the autumn they showed a lively interest in the policy to be expected from Canning. Cuba, however, was now the chief source of international complication. In June, 1819, Rush had received from Castlereagh the assurance that his Government had no intention of annexing it. Each power, however, was far from trusting the other. The Cabinet of Monroe was full of suspicion of Great Britain, and Calhoun in particular thought it expedient to make sacrifices to bind her not to take Cuba or Texas. Their fears were heightened by the belief, indignantly refuted by Spain, that the island would be ceded to Great Britain. On the other hand, Stratford Canning was constantly urged by the Foreign Secretary to find some proof that the United States cherished designs against it. Both joined in doubting France. Each had much at stake. The possessor of Cuba would be the powerful neighbour of Jamaica and of the Bahama group. The interest of the United States was summed up in the dictum of Jefferson that the acquisition of Cuba would complete their national wellbeing. In spite of their professions of neutrality towards Spain, and in spite of their renunciations in London, the state of the island strongly tempted the Administration. Tranquillity, when it existed, was maintained only by the strength of the Governor. A strong government alone could protect the numerous American residents, and extirpate the pirates, who were the pest of American commerce. Above all, there was in Cuba a genuine movement for admission into the Union. The British Consul-General at the Havana had for years reported that the Creoles were devoted to this idea. A section of them made definite proposals to the United States, and in September 1822, the Cabinet long discussed the matter. The sober Calhoun endorsed Jefferson's opinion that Cuba was worth an English war. To Adams, on the other hand, it was plain that at that time such a war would end in the possession of the island by Great Britain. Eventually, therefore, it was decided to wait and watch, in the hope that the Cubans would achieve independence by themselves.

In the summer of 1823, then, the foreign politics of the United States were chiefly concerned with Cuba and the far north-west. In the latter question also Great Britain had interests at stake. From her ambassador at St Petersburg, as from other foreign diplomatists, Russia was compelled to seek protection for vessels entering the regions in which the Czar had declared himself supreme. The Ukase of 1821, moreover, maintained the imperial sovereignty over territory which had formed the subject of a convention between Great Britain and the United States. Both powers, therefore, deemed it advantageous that the whole question should be settled by a triangular negotiation at St Petersburg, and it was accordingly withdrawn from the list of subjects discussed in December, 1823, by Huskisson, Stratford Canning, Rush and Gallatin, at the office of the Board of Trade. In July, however, Adams had sent to St Petersburg and London general instructions with regard to the Pacific boundary of the United States, the principles of which anticipate that part of the Monroe Doctrine which treats of colonisation.

Hence at the time when it becomes necessary to study in detail the actual composition of the President's message, the Administration had for six years pursued a policy of peace and patriotism. Standing absolutely aloof from the quarrels of the Old World, they had shown in the questions of Florida, of Cuba, of the north-west, and of America south of their own borders, that they would pursue their own interests regardless of European dictation. Their relations with Great Britain, relations which had improved into something approaching concert, had been governed by the same determination. While their intercourse with the individual powers of the European continent had been friendly, the collective principles of the Holy Alliance stood in marked contrast to their own. The battle-ground of conflicting opinions was South America, and the cry of the United States was the Message of Monroe.

CHAPTER IV.

THE DIPLOMACY OF 1823.

To study the immediate formation of the Message, we must examine transactions in Washington and in London. On one side of the Atlantic, George Canning was negotiating with Richard Rush, the Minister of the United States, while on the other, Monroe and Adams were preparing for the autumn meetings of the Cabinet. The existence of a representative of Great Britain at Washington has usually been overlooked. Before leaving for England in August, Stratford Canning had presented as *charge d'affaires* his Secretary of Legation, Mr Henry Unwin Addington, who for two years performed his duties with such diligence as to win the approbation of his Government at the expense of his health. Throughout the time at which the Presidential Message was being drafted, he was in constant communication with the Secretary of State, and his despatches give an unique picture of the workings of the Administration as seen from the outside. From the point of view of Canning, the diplomacy in London has been outlined by Mr A. G. Stapleton, his secretary and apologist. Written within six years of the Monroe

Message, his narrative is authentic rather than voluminous. The American side of the negotiations, on
the other hand, was presented later, but with far more
detail, by Rush himself. Meanwhile Adams was
writing in his Diary day by day the history of the
interviews and cabinet councils at which the policy
of the United States was discussed and determined,
and at every stage Addington was plying him with
questions and filling bulky despatches with the replies.
Read in the light of previous history, the combination
of the four accounts seems to present a fairly complete
record of the birth of the Monroe Doctrine.

On the 16th August, Rush, while still awaiting
instructions on the subject of the north-western
boundary, held an interview with Canning in which
the conversation turned towards the danger from
France to the constitutional cause in Spain. The
American Minister took the opportunity of recalling
the sentiments of Canning's despatch of March 31st
to Sir Charles Stuart, the British Ambassador at Paris.
Great Britain, he pointed out, had there disclaimed all
intention of appropriating any Spanish colony, and had
declared herself satisfied that France would exercise
similar self-restraint. Canning replied by enquiring
what the Government of the United States would be
likely to say to going hand in hand with England in
such a policy. Concert of *action*, he thought, would
not be called for. Great Britain, though she would
never again attempt to aid in the making up of the
quarrel between Spain and her colonies, would not
oppose a settlement effected in a spirit of preference
to the mother-country. She had as yet taken no steps

towards recognising the new republics, but was about to send a commission of enquiry to Mexico.

Rush was careful to express no opinion either in favour of or against the suggestion. Four days later he received a private and confidential note which developed it. In the words of Stapleton,

"The English Government, said Mr Canning, had nothing to disguise on the subject.

1. It conceived the recovery of the Colonies by Spain to be hopeless.

·2. It conceived the question of the recognition of them to be one of time and circumstances.

3. It was, however, by no means disposed to throw any impediment in the way of an arrangement between them and the mother-country by amicable negotiation.   ·

4. It aimed not at the possession of any portion of them for Great Britain.

5. And, it could not see any part of them transferred to any other power with indifference.

"These were its opinions and feelings; and if they were shared by the Government of the United States, 'Why,' asked Mr Canning, 'should they not be mutually confided to each other, and declared in the face of the world? Was Mr Rush authorized to enter into any negotiation, and to sign any convention upon the subject? or would he exchange Ministerial notes upon it? A proceeding of such a nature,' continued Mr Canning, 'would be at once the most effectual and the least offensive mode of intimating the joint disapprobation of Great Britain and the United States, of any projects, which might be cherished by any

European power, of a forcible enterprize for reducing the Colonies to subjugation on the behalf, or in the name of Spain; or of the acquisition of any part of them to itself by cession or by conquest.'"

The confidential answer of August 23rd, which seemed at the time "in every respect highly creditable to its distinguished author," is described by Rush himself. The United States he could safely say, agreed with Great Britain in regarding the recovery of the Colonies by Spain as hopeless, in the determination not to oppose any amicable arrangement which should end the war, and in the denial of all intention to acquire territory in Spanish America. Having recognised the Colonies as independent States, they desired to see them received into the family of nations, especially by Great Britain. "And last," he maintained, "we should regard as unjust, and fruitful of highly disastrous consequences, any attempt on the part of any European Power to take possession of them by conquest, by cession, or on any other ground or pretext." His instructions and powers, however, said nothing which could authorise him to publish these sentiments in writing. That he was able, from the general directions of Adams, to win the hearty approval of Monroe in saying so much as this, shows how far the policy of the Administration, as interpreted by the Secretary of State, had already advanced towards the Monroe Doctrine. To his own Government he justified his caution by pointing out the danger of becoming implicated in "the federative system of Europe," and of taking any step which might prove exceptionable in the eyes of France. From Canning's tone of earnestness, none the less, he inferred that the British Cabinet feared that France, alone or in conjunction with the allied powers, meditated ambitious enterprises against the independence of the new Spanish-American States.

Three days later, his surmise was confirmed by a second confidential communication from Canning. France, it was pointed out, expected very speedily to achieve her military objects in Spain. "England had received notice, though not such as imposed the necessity of instant action," that, as soon as this was done, "a proposal would be made for a congress in Europe, or some other concert and consultation, specifically on the affairs of Spanish America." Rush found himself warranted by his instructions in replying immediately in words which still more clearly anticipate the Monroe Doctrine. His Government, he said, "would regard as objectionable any interference whatever in the affairs of Spanish America, unsolicited by the late provinces themselves and against their will. It would regard the convening of a congress to deliberate upon their affairs, as a measure uncalled-for, and indicative of a policy highly unfriendly to the tranquillity of the world. It could never look with insensibility upon such an exercise of European jurisdiction over communities now of right exempt from it, and entitled to regulate their own concerns unmolested from abroad." Canning again replied without delay, though his letter did not reach its destination till September 7th. While professing himself grateful for the cordial spirit in which his communication had been received, he regretted that the Minister of the United States could not undertake to decide upon any

R.   4 formal proposition without previous reference to his Government. During the time necessary for communication with the United States, the progress of events might rob the proposed co-operation of its value, while Great Britain would be trammelled in any other mode of expressing her views. Rush was thereby confirmed in his resolution to accede to the overtures only in case Great Britain would yield the point of recognition. This concession, he informed his Government, he would continue to urge, though not in such fashion as to alienate an administration "as favourably disposed towards the United States as any that could be formed."

The language of Stapleton suggests that after receiving the reply to his first proposals, Canning "allowed the matter to drop," and turned at once to the French ambassador, Prince Polignac. Rush, however, shows that a double rebuff did not end the matter. On returning to London in the middle of September, Canning sought an interview, and renewed his arguments in favour of co-operation in a matter which he represented as increasingly urgent. Five weeks before, he had spoken of the commission to Mexico, and now he was able to announce that consuls to the new states would soon be appointed. To a demonstration of the importance of the step proposed, as implicating the United States in European affairs, and departing from their traditional policy, he replied in words that might well make Adams "singularly cheerful and complaisant." If the policy was new, he argued, so also was the problem, "and full as much American as European, to say no more.... The United States...were the first

power established on that continent, and now con-
fessedly the leading power.... Could Europe expect
this indifference?" The Minister of the United States
received with the utmost caution this lesson in the
first principles of the Monroe Doctrine. "There might
be room for thinking," he admitted, "that the late
formation of these new states in our hemisphere would
impose new political duties upon the United States,
not merely as coupled with the great cause of national
freedom, but as closely connected also with their own
present and future interests, and even the very existence, finally, of their own institutions." This question,
however, the Government must decide. Canning
pressed the point still further. Prevention was better
than cure, and delay might mar all. The interest of
the United States was regarded by Great Britain as of
such importance that she would reserve to herself the
option of refusing to attend any conference on South
America at which their representative should not be
present. Rush's reply was a bid for recognition. If
Great Britain would formally acknowledge the independence which by her own confession the new states
had substantially acquired, he would stand upon his
general powers as Minister plenipotentiary, and sign
the declaration proposed. That their internal stability
was uncertain, he could not deny. Recognition, however, would remedy it. Independence was a settled
question; and, in negotiating with Great Britain and
Russia on the subject of the Pacific coast, the United
States would be obliged to assume it. He saw, however, that his arguments could not prevail, and con-
tented himself with a resolution not to attend any

4—2

conference on South America. A week later, Canning offered a promise of the future recognition of the young republics, but only thereby exposed himself to a fourth refusal. Early in October, he arranged for a general negotiation between Great Britain and the United States, and took the opportunity of informing Rush that the consuls were very soon to set out for Spanish America. With the offer of September 26th, however, his communications ceased to directly influence the formation of the President's Message.

Having thus failed to secure the co-operation of the United States, Canning determined to inform the French Government directly that an attack on Spanish America would be followed by war with Great Britain. On the 9th October, therefore, he met Polignac, with the object of exchanging communications on the subject. The importance of their interview is attested by the wide dissemination of the Memorandum which embodied its results. Valuable as formulating the policy of both powers, its most striking feature is the renunciation by France of any intention to assist Spain against the colonies, or to acquire exclusive commercial advantages for herself. Had it been made known to the Cabinet of Monroe, therefore, it could not have failed to exercise an effect on the construction and on the value of the President's Message. The world which the Monroe Doctrine defied was, for purposes of aggression against South America, equivalent to France and Russia. If then the declaration of Polignac were construed at Washington as withdrawing France merely for the moment, Russia alone would remain, and Russia, as Canning held, could hardly act alone.

From Rush's account of his "full and final interview" with Canning on the 24th November, however,
it is clear that no details of the Polignac conference
had reached him before that time. Canning then read
to him the Memorandum, but allowed him no copy
until fully a month later; when he promised to trans-
mit it to his Government "wholly as a confidential
paper." It is difficult to believe that Canning would
have so long refused an official document to the
representative of a power whose friendship he was
anxious to retain, had it been possible for him or for
his Government to have obtained it from some other
source. It is equally difficult to see what that source
could have been. The other Ministers of the United
States in Europe were wont to communicate to their
colleague in London any news of special importance.
Although, therefore, the Memorandum was sent on
October 13th to Sir William A'Court at Madrid, and
although on November 19th he reports that it had
been sent in a circular despatch to French diplomatic
agents, it seems at least improbable that it could have
reached Washington in time to influence the Cabinet
Councils which ended on November 26th. In conversation with the French premier at the beginning of
1824, the British ambassador at Paris upheld this
view. Canning himself asserted that the French
Government preceded him in the dissemination of the
paper, and Chateaubriand recorded the fact that on
the 1st November it was discussed by the Council and
forwarded to the French ambassadors at Berlin, Vienna
and St Petersburg. The argument is strengthened by
the silence of Adams's Diary with regard to it. From

November 7th, before which it could not well have arrived at Washington, to November 27th, when the composition of the Message may be regarded as complete, the events of each day are described with exceptional fulness. Nothing is said, however, of the receipt of any account of the conference, or of the use in the Cabinet of any arguments based upon it. On the hypothesis that it had been communicated, the omission, as also the extraordinary dejection of the President noticed in the middle of November, is not easily intelligible. If, on the other hand, the Memorandum arrived after November 27th, the silence may without difficulty be accounted for. When once the decision of the Administration had been arrived at, any supplementary information which might have assisted in reaching it would become of comparatively small account. Adams, too, was being plunged into the thick of the struggle for the Presidency, and his Diary bears witness to the fact. Of the actual reception of the Message by Congress he says not a word, but records that during the month of March he has received 235 visitors. The balance of probability, therefore, seems to indicate that Monroe and Adams shared the ignorance of Rush and Addington, and that the conference between Canning and Polignac exercised no influence on the formulation of the Monroe Doctrine.

Rush's reports of the proposals made to him by Canning reached the United States during the summer recess. The President thought the occasion of such importance as to warrant him in consulting Jefferson and Madison ; and at the end of October the aged statesmen sent him their advice. The correspondence which had taken place in England during the month of August is described by the former as " more important than anything that has happened since our Revolution." Highly as he valued the chance of obtaining Cuba, he advised the President to renounce everything in order to pledge Great Britain to oppose the Holy Alliance. Madison's answer was less decided in tone. Viewing dispassionately the conduct of Great Britain and the circumstances under which the offer was made, he could not avoid the conclusion that it was impelled more by her interest than by a principle of general liberty. This had from the first been the opinion of Adams, and, in a less degree, of Monroe. Where Canning had claimed that his plan would be " expedient for themselves and beneficial to the world," every American statesman read ' expedient for, and beneficial to Great Britain.'

In the first days of November, Addington received from the Secretary of State at a dinner party an account of the original interview between Canning and Rush. " Mr Adams," he wrote, " seemed extremely gratified, and evidently contemplated his country as already placed by it on a much higher elevation than that on which she had hitherto stood." Shortly before this time, indeed, he had held a conversation with Adams, which he had reported to Canning in a despatch dated, it seems probable, November 3rd. A marginal note to the reply affords evidence that the subject was a "joint manifesto on Spanish America." The proceedings, however, were considered by Canning of so confidential a nature as to be unfit for official communication. Early in December, therefore, he took

the strong measure of withdrawing the despatch and
sending it back to Addington to be put into the form
of a private and confidential letter. It may perhaps be
conjectured that towards the end of September Canning
had striven to effect by diplomacy at Washington what
he had failed to accomplish in London, and that in a
private letter he had instructed the British *charge* to
seek an interview with the Secretary of State. The
unbroken sequence of Addington's subsequent despatches on what he terms 'the same subject,' in any
case, renders it improbable that any vital point of
Adams's communication has been lost.

Early in November, the President returned to the
capital, and summoned the Cabinet to begin its deliberations. The illness of Crawford had removed one source
of disagreement, and for more than a fortnight the
only Ministers present were Adams, Calhoun and
Southard, the Secretary of the Navy. On November
7th, the propositions of Canning to Rush and the
designs of the Holy Alliance upon South America
formed the subject of a long and general discussion.
Calhoun's opinion was that of Jefferson ; but Adams
pleaded with vigour and success that the United States
should preserve entire freedom of action. No voice
was raised in favour of sending a representative to any
conference on the affairs of South America, while all
agreed that a Minister should immediately be accredited
to France. President and Secretary of State were of
one mind in spurning any position subordinate to that
of Great Britain, and, amid general acquiescence, the
latter claimed that the Czar's lecture on Legitimacy
should be met by a declaration of United States

principles addressed to Russia and to France. After the meeting, he won the approval of the President to the idea of making this communication and the refusal of the overtures of Great Britain " parts of a combined system of policy and adapted to each other." Less than a month before its appearance, therefore, the Monroe Doctrine had assumed no more definite shape.

The result of the Cabinet council was manifest in the haughtiness with which Adams next day addressed the Ambassador of the Czar, and in the profuse cordiality with which he received Addington two days later. Scarcely had he caught sight of the British *charge*, before he had begun to read aloud the whole of the communications between Canning and Rush. To the condemnation by Great Britain of foreign interference in trans-Atlantic affairs he signified his entire and cordial assent, and approved no less of Rush's statement that British recognition of Spanish America was indispensable to concert with the United States. The voluminous report of the conference of September 19th next gave him occasion for self-congratulation. " He spoke loftily," writes Addington, "of the announcement which had already, on a former occasion, been made to some of the European powers, more especially Russia, of the United States considering the whole American Continent to be composed of independent nations. and of the intention of this country to oppose any future attempts at colonizing North or South America by European Powers. This announcement, he said, was more especially directed against Russia and her North West Pacific schemes." To Addington's appeal for a speedy decision on the proposal of Great Britain " he

replied that that measure was of such magnitude, such
paramount consequence as involving the whole future
policy of the United States, as far at least as regarded
their own hemisphere, that the President was anxious
to give it the most deliberate consideration, and to take
the sense of his whole Cabinet upon it."

The complacency of the Administration, however,
was disturbed by the news that Cadiz had fallen.
Monroe and Calhoun were plunged into the depths of
dejection, and feared that the Holy Alliance would
immediately restore all South America to Spain. Their
alarm was shared by the public, and the tide of popular
feeling turned in favour of Great Britain. Adams
alone remained firm, and called on the President either
to accept or decline Canning's proposals. On the 15th
of November the question was thrashed out in the
Cabinet, and Calhoun's idea of leaving the reply of the
United States to the discretion of their representative
in London gave rise to much discussion. At last
Adams, perhaps not uninfluenced by his belief that
Rush had risen too rapidly, prevailed on his colleagues
to "bring the whole answer to a test of right and
wrong. Considering the South Americans as independent nations," he argued, "they themselves, and no
other nation, had the *right* to dispose of their condition." No agreement on the part of any number of
foreign powers could warrant them in impairing this
right to national independence. Next day, further
dispatches from London showed Rush's disappointment
at Canning's change of tone, and on the 17th, when
Adams drafted a general reply, there could be little
doubt as to its tenour. In the President's opinion,

Canning had been offered some inducements to quiet his apprehensions, while the Secretary of State was more than ever convinced that he had feigned alarm in the hope of surprising the United States into a guarantee of Cuba to Spain.

On the same day, Addington paid a further visit to the Department of State. Nothing more, Adams informed him, had passed in London, and the President's final decision would probably be taken as soon as Crawford should be well enough to attend the Cabinet. Before the United States and Great Britain could act in common, he went on to explain, it was indispensable that the latter should admit the principle of colonial independence by recognizing one or more of the new states. His words show what he regarded as the result of the test of right and wrong, and explain the principle on which the second part of the Monroe Doctrine was based. "The United States, having acknowledged the independence of the trans-Atlantic territories, had a *right* to object to the interference of foreign powers in the affairs of those territories. To Great Britain it might be objected that, although possessing the *option*, she had no distinct *right* so to do. She regarded those territories as still dependencies of Spain, and in that character she might allow not only Spain, but *pro re nata* other powers, as allies of Spain, to interpose in reducing them by force to obedience. Such a proceeding was impossible to the United States, from the mere fact of their recognition of the independence of the territories in question." Their action with regard to insular Spain, if it should exercise its inherent right to independence, would be governed by the same principles. They would never admit a right on the part of any third power to interfere in subjugating the colonies for Spain, or on the part of Spain, to cede them to another power.

The assured spirit of which these words were full contrasted strongly with the dejection of the President and the apprehensions of the people. The journals feared for the liberties even of their own portion of the western world, and the public was inclined to build too great hopes on the appointment of British consuls to South America. The authoritative *National Intelligencer*, in particular, announced that England's best and most influential statesmen were well aware that English freedom and American independence were equally hateful to those who would enslave Europe. At the end of the month a general impression seemed prevalent that the moment would arrive and would be welcome when Great Britain and the United States, as chiefs of the constitutional cause in either hemisphere, would join hands in support of it. All were resolved that in the United States, at least, the arm of despotism should not be raised.

On the 19th of November, Addington once more received from Adams a greeting of "unusual affability." The instructions to Rush, he was informed, were delayed by the deliberation of the President on what was characterised for the second time as "the most delicate and important measure of his whole administration." The necessity of a common basis of principle was still further demonstrated, and the peculiar views of the United States once more explained. Having acknowledged the new states as independent, they had become incapable of admitting that other powers could acquire the right to interfere. Though it was difficult to see how Great Britain could break off her former strict relations with the other allies of Spain, the United States would probably decline to attend any conference on South America, unless, as they intended to suggest, the new republics were also invited to be present. No congress could give Europe a right " to stretch the arm of power across the Atlantic for the purpose of subjugating independent states...The very atmosphere of such an assembly must be considered by this Government as infected, and unfit for their plenipotentiary to breathe in."

One week before the language of the President was finally decided, therefore, the Administration may be regarded as having settled its policy from the negative, but not from the positive point of view. All its members understood that they had recognised the South American republics as independent states. They would impugn their own good faith by countenancing any attempt to destroy that independence on the ground that it had not been fully achieved. This, however, must be the ground taken by Spain, should she find means to renew the war, or by the Holy Allies, should they decide to interfere. Such interference, therefore, must be repugnant to the United States, and no envoy of theirs should be suspected of lending it sanction. Nor could they connive at the denial of the rights of the new states involved in any attempt to found colonial establishments within their borders. They were resolved to uphold their own claim to the north-west against the Ukase of the Czar. As to Cuba, all were of opinion that it would be greatly to the detriment of the United States if the island should pass into the hands of France or of Great Britain. There, however, the question of principle—of the right of every people to choose its own government—had not yet been raised. Its present condition was tranquil, and Great Britain, which had solemnly disclaimed all intention of acquiring it for herself, would not be likely to permit France to profit by her abstinence. It remained, therefore, for Monroe and his Cabinet to decide what active measures should be taken to ward off the danger of European aggression which threatened the new republics, and which might eventually affect the United States also.

The means readiest to hand lay in an acceptance of the proposals made by Canning. Washington, however, had forbidden his successors to commit their country to entangling alliances with Europe. It was suspected, moreover, that a common declaration against deriving advantages from the struggle, or against allowing other powers to take part in it, would commit the United States too far, and Great Britain not far enough. The former would renounce their chance of ultimately acceding to the petition of Cuba and Texas to be admitted into the Union, and would divide their claim to the gratitude of the states which they had been the first to recognise. Above all, they feared to humiliate themselves by conforming to the wishes of Great Britain, the power which the Cabinet, as Democrats, viewed with most jealousy, and with which, since the Declaration of Independence, their country had passed one-fifth of its existence at war. Although, therefore, Monroe was inclined to empower Rush to act in concert with the British Government in case of any sudden danger, Adams stoutly maintained that nothing should be left to his discretion. In the Cabinet of November the 21st he gained his point. He also defeated the President's amendment in favour of accepting an arrangement by which special privileges, or even a restoration of authority, might be conceded by the revolted colonies to Spain. The final draft of the instructions to Rush claimed that the United States should be treated by the South Americans upon the footing of equality with the most favoured nation, and was, Adams states, conformable to his own views. He next secured more explicit approval for the project of the manifesto to Russia, which had been generally acquiesced in a fortnight before. He desired moderately but firmly to declare the dissent of the United States from the principles championed by the Czar, and to assert those upon which their own government was founded. The lineaments of the Monroe Doctrine seem to be discernible in his proposal " while disclaiming all intention of attempting to propagate them by force, and all interference with the political affairs of Europe, to declare our expectation and hope that the European powers will equally abstain from the attempt to spread their principles in the American hemisphere, or to subjugate by force any part of these continents to their will."

The President, having approved of the idea, proceeded to read to the Cabinet the portions of his message already drafted. In the tone of " deep solemnity and high alarm" with which it began, traces of his previous, dejection might be perceived. The country, he declared, was menaced by foreign powers. He censured both the principles and the practice of the French invasion of Spain, and recommended an appropriation for a Minister to be sent to the Greeks. Calhoun, regarding the attack on popular principles as unprecedented, approved the whole. Adams, on the other hand, impugned both the policy of alarm and the facts on which it was based; and, next day, implored the President to avoid anything like aggression. The United States, he argued, might have been hasty in recognising the Spanish colonies as independent. By the consequences of that action, indeed, they must abide, but why defy the Allies in the heart of Europe? "The ground that I wish to take," he writes in his Diary, "is that of earnest remonstrance against the interference of the European powers by force with South America, but to disclaim all interference on our part with Europe; to make up an American cause, and adhere inflexibly to that."

Sunday passed, and on Monday he was gratified to find that the President had accepted his advice. Next day, the Cabinet met again, this time with the addition of Wirt, the Attorney-General, a friend of Madison and Monroe, and a man of the strongest common sense. The subject of discussion was the manifesto to Russia and to the world, which Adams claimed to have drawn to correspond exactly with the paragraph in which the President had embodied his recommendations. He describes it in words which seem to depict the Monroe Doctrine when full grown. Besides answering the exhortations of Alexander and the proposals of Canning, it was, according to its author, "meant to be eventually an exposition of the principles of this Government, and a brief development of its political system as henceforth to be maintained;—essentially republican,...essentially pacific,...but declaring that, having recognised the independence of the South American states, we could not see with indifference any attempt by European powers, by forcible interposition, either to restore the Spanish dominion on the American continents, or to introduce monarchical principles into those countries, or to transfer any portion of the ancient or present possessions of Spain to any other European power."

The manifesto thus drawn up was defended by its author against a running fire of criticism. Calhoun doubted the need for it, and Monroe feared lest its republicanism should so shock Great Britain that the Holy Alliance might be enabled to buy back her support. Wirt raised the most important point of all by enquiring "if the Holy Allies *should* act in direct hostility against South America, whether this country would oppose them by war?" In reply, Adams urged that his declaration did not pledge the United States to "absolute war," and that Great Britain was already more committed than themselves. The interest of each of the Allies, again, would be injured by the restoration of South America to Spain. Even if they could agree on a treaty of partition, they could only offer Cuba to Great Britain, and this neither they nor Spain would consent to give her. His reliance upon the co-operation of Great Britain rested, not upon her principles but her interest. Her principles, however, would not be outraged, and his " whole paper was drawn up to come in conclusion precisely to the identical declaration of Mr Canning himself, and to express our concurrence with it."

Next day the battle was renewed, and for four hours raged round the President's draft and the corresponding manifesto proposed by Adams. The gist of the whole question, according to the latter, was how far the United States ought to take their stand against the Holy Alliance in defence of South America. Wirt declared that the feeling in favour of the revolutionists was not general, and that it was inexpedient to be perhaps ensnared by Canning into declarations against the Holy Alliance without first consulting Congress. Calhoun maintained his opinion that, for their own sake, the United States must detach Great Britain from the Allies. He therefore favoured the Message as proclaiming United States principles in the sanctuary of their own fire-side, but thought that the manifesto would be deeply offensive to the Holy Alliance, and also to the monarchical government of Great Britain. In reply to these strictures, Adams poured forth his wonted wealth of argument. On the previous day he had shown that the Holy Alliance was not likely to reconquer South America. Now, however, he drew a vivid picture of the new states partitioned out among the powers. " What would be our situation," he asked, "England holding Cuba; France, Mexico?" The French might even recover Louisiana, and the United States could not too soon take steps to repel the danger. If, on the other hand, they should shrink from action, Great Britain, by her command of the sea, might triumph over the Holy Alliance single-handed, and so make South America a protectorate of her own. By sanctioning his manifesto, moreover, the Executive did not—as, indeed, by law it could not—commit the nation to war. Canning himself had stated from the first that his object was merely a concerted expression of sentiment, which, he supposed, would render it unnecessary to appeal to arms. From his personal knowledge of Alexander, again, Adams did not believe that his draft would give him offence. "As the Holy Alliance had come to edify and instruct us with their principles," he maintained, "it was due in candor to them and in justice to ourselves, to return them the compliment."

Having thus borne down the opposition to his plan, he proceeded to defend its details. The President, however, by insisting that Rush should not finally refuse co-operation without recognition, showed that his principles were less extreme. With regard to the manifesto, he reserved judgment till next day. He then advised the omission of the paragraphs to which the Cabinet had raised objections. All Adams's powers of logic and of entreaty had to be called into play before he would consent to re-examine the exposition of the principles of the United States—the foundation of the whole. Later in the day, the victory was won. Thwarted at every point by his more vigorous lieutenant, the President sent a note "expressing," according to Adams, "the apprehension that the paragraph of principles contained a *direct* attack upon the Holy Allies, by a statement of principles which they had violated, but yet consenting that I should re-insert the paragraph, on account of the importance that I attached to it."

In this way, Adams secured the adoption of the system of policy of which the presidential Message was a single expression. The story of its evolution illustrates the evolution of the Monroe Doctrine. Adams alone held firmly to principles which, perhaps, no other member of the Administration fully understood. He was able to predict to the representative of Columbia that his countrymen would soon see the deep interest taken by the United States in the maintenance of their independence. On the eve of the Message itself, Addington received his assurances that "the United States would show by facts how cordially they concurred in the line of policy to be pursued by Great Britain." The instructions to Rush and Middleton would soon be drawn up and despatched. "He concluded," says the British representative, "by expressing in terms of warmth and apparent sincerity, his earnest hope that the relations which existed between our two Governments would become daily of a closer and a more confidential nature."

CHAPTER V.

THE AUTHORSHIP OF THE MONROE DOCTRINE.

EXPERIENCE of the first four years of Monroe's presidency had enabled his Secretary of State to write in 1820, " The composition of these messages is upon a uniform plan. They begin with general remarks upon the condition of the country, noticing recent occurrences of material importance, passing encomiums upon our form of government, paying due homage to the sovereign power of the people, and turning to account every topic which can afford a paragraph of public gratulation; then pass in review the foreign affairs; the circumstances of our relations with the principal powers of Europe; then, looking inwards, adverting to the state of the finances, the revenues, public expenditures, debts and land sales, the progress of fortifications and naval armaments, with a few words about the Indians, and a few about the slave-trade."

With a detail which the President excused as necessary to the opening of a new Congress, almost all these subjects find a place in the Message of December 2nd, 1823. Two passages, however, collectively termed the Monroe Doctrine, have won wider

fame than the rest. In the review of foreign affairs
it is stated that:

"At the proposal of the Russian Imperial Government, made through the minister of the Emperor
residing here, a full power and instructions have been
transmitted to the minister of the United States at
St Petersburg, to arrange, by amicable negotiation,
the respective rights and interests of the two nations
on the north-west coast of this continent. A similar
proposal had been made by his Imperial Majesty to the
Government of Great Britain, which has likewise been
acceded to. The government of the United States
has been desirous, by this friendly proceeding, of
manifesting the great value which they have invariably
attached to the friendship of the Emperor, and their
solicitude to cultivate the best understanding with his
government. In the discussions to which this interest
has given rise and in the arrangements by which they
may terminate, the occasion has been judged proper
for asserting, as a principle in which the rights and
interests of the United States are involved, that the
American continents, by the free and independent condition which they have assumed and maintain, are
henceforth not to be considered as subjects for future
colonization by any European powers."

The Message then treats of other foreign relations,
of finance, of the army and navy, of posts and tariffs,
and of the vexed question of internal improvements.
It expresses the warm sympathy of the United States
with the Greeks in their struggle to "resume their
equal station among the nations of the earth." The
remainder, with the exception of a peroration on the

progress of the United States and on their Constitution, reads as follows :

"It was stated at the commencement of the last session that a great effort was then, making in Spain and Portugal to improve the condition of the people of those countries, and that it appeared to be conducted with extraordinary moderation. It need scarcely be remarked that the result has been so far very different from what was then anticipated. Of events in that quarter of the globe, with which we have so much intercourse and from which we derive our origin, we have always been anxious and interested spectators. The citizens of the United States cherish sentiments the most friendly in favor of the liberty and happiness of their fellow men on that side of the Atlantic. In the wars of the European powers, in matters relating to themselves, we have never taken any part, nor does it comport with our policy to do so. It is only when our rights are invaded or seriously menaced, that we resent injuries or make preparation for our defence. With the movements in this hemisphere we are, of necessity, more immediately connected, and by causes which must be obvious to all enlightened and impartial observers. The political system of the allied powers is essentially different in this respect from that of America. This difference proceeds from that which exists in their respective governments. And to the defence of our own, which has been achieved by the loss of so much blood and treasure, and matured by the wisdom of their most enlightened citizens, and under which we have enjoyed unexampled felicity, this whole nation is devoted. We owe it, therefore, to

candor and to the amicable relations existing between
the United States and those powers to declare that
we should consider any attempt on their part to extend
their system to any portion of this hemisphere as
dangerous to our peace and safety. With the existing
colonies or dependencies of any European power we
have not interfered, and shall not interfere. But with
the Governments who have declared their independence
and maintained it, and whose independence we have,
on great consideration and on just principles, acknowledged, we could not view any interposition for the
purpose of oppressing them, or controlling in any other
manner their destiny, by any European power, in any
other light than as the manifestation of an unfriendly
disposition towards the United States. In the war
between those new Governments and Spain we declared
our neutrality at the time of their recognition, and
to this we have adhered and shall continue to adhere,
provided no change shall occur which, in the judgment
of the competent authorities of this Government, shall
make a corresponding change on the part of the United
States indispensable to their security.

"The late events in Spain and Portugal show that
Europe is still unsettled. Of this important fact no
stronger proof can be adduced than that the allied
powers should have thought it proper, on a principle
satisfactory to themselves, to have interposed by force
in the internal concerns of Spain. To what extent
such interposition may be carried on the same principle,
is a question to which all independent powers, whose
Governments differ from theirs, are interested; even
those most remote, and surely none more so than

the United States. Our policy in regard to Europe, which was adopted at an early stage of the wars which have so long agitated that quarter of the globe, nevertheless remains the same, which is, not to interfere in the internal concerns of any of its powers; to consider the Government *de facto* as the legitimate Government for us; to cultivate friendly relations with it, and to preserve those relations by a frank, firm, and manly policy; meeting, in all instances, the just claims of every power, submitting to injuries from none. But in regard to these continents, circumstances are eminently and conspicuously different. It is impossible that the allied powers should extend their political system to any portion of either continent without endangering our peace and happiness; nor can anyone believe that our southern brethren, if left to themselves, would adopt it of their own accord. It is equally impossible, therefore, that we should behold such interposition, in any form, with indifference. If we look to the comparative strength and resources of Spain and those new Governments, and their distance from each other, it must be obvious that she can never subdue them. It is still the true policy of the United States to leave the parties to themselves, in the hope that other powers will pursue the same course."

The process by which it was decided that the policy which these passages express should be adopted by the United States and declared by the President has been examined in the preceding chapter. The examination has at least sufficed to show that, from whatever quarter may have come the impulse to pronounce the Monroe Doctrine, its formulation cannot be sought

outside the Cabinet. The connection of Canning with
the Doctrine of which he has often been termed the
author has been exposed. The part played by Jefferson,
on whose behalf also a claim has been put forward,
seems to be denned in the fact that his advice was
sought and was not followed. It remains to discover,
if possible, to whose hand were due the phrases actually
employed. The Cabinet which considered the presidential Message consisted of five members, and it is
impossible to suppose that Calhoun, Southard, or Wirt
shaped its foreign policy or drafted its conclusions.
The problem, therefore, reduces itself to a decision
between the claims of the President and of the
Secretary of State.

This special question of authorship, indeed, is of
more than speculative importance. The whole history
of the Monroe Doctrine, and its recent history most of
all, shows that its literal interpretation is far from
clear. Phrases which in the mouth of one man might
be the obscure expression of confused thought, would
not be uttered by another without a deep political
meaning. Once at least, Monroe had to enquire of
Adams the meaning of a paragraph drawn by himself
in his own words, and it is desirable to spare a new
generation the toil of reading into the Message of 1823
ideas which it was never intended to convey. The historical estimate of the succeeding Administration and of
its head, moreover, must depend in great measure on
the verdict. If the words of the Monroe Doctrine were
the vehicle chosen by Adams to convey his political
ideas, new light is thrown on his Panama Messages,
and new judgment must be pronounced on their author.

The Doctrine, again, it may safely be conjectured, derives much claim to popular veneration from its supposed parentage by Monroe. Even while he continued to hold the reins of state, men felt that the halcyon days of the Republic had arrived. History has proved their instinct true, and after seventy years the centre of the whole is the mild and venerable patriarch of whom little but good is known, and who may the more easily be reputed a hero. If, on the other hand, the Monroe Doctrine were proved to be the offspring of Adams, much of the glamour encircling it might fade away, and its interpretation might pass more completely from the sphere of sentiment into that of reason. Direct documentary evidence is unhappily wanting. Adams made his claim, if anywhere, between the lines of his Diary, which described the deliberations by which the Message was preceded. The title of Monroe, on the other hand, seems to rest on the fact that he penned the words despatched by him to Congress. "Very little has come under my eye," says his biographer, in speaking of the Doctrine, "to illustrate the workings of Monroe's mind." "If memoranda of Monroe's upon this subject are still extant they have eluded me." The remaining members of the Cabinet, with the doubtful exception of Calhoun, have forborne to lift the veil. It is necessary therefore, for the most part, to supplement the evidence of the Diary with arguments based on probability,—on the power of the two men to produce the Doctrine, and on the extent to which its principles agree with theirs.

Though the denunciations against European colonisation and European interference have been confounded by patriots into a single dogma that America is for the Americans, or, as some would say, for the citizens of the United States, a glance at the Message itself will suffice to show that the two are not at first sight connected. Historical enquiry proves that their origin was likewise separate. The former—the quotation by the President of a principle assumed by the United States in their recent territorial negotiations with Russia, "that the American continents, by the free and independent condition which they have assumed and maintained, are henceforth not to be considered as subjects for future colonisation by any European powers"—had not been the subject of the recent Cabinet deliberations. The silence of the Diary is on this point confirmed by the statement of Calhoun, made in combating the principle after a quarter of a century had elapsed, of his impression that this portion of the Message originated with Adams. The gist of it had for months, indeed, been familiar to the Ministers of the United States in foreign courts. In the middle of July, Adams had informed the Russian Ambassador that throughout the forthcoming negotiations on the Ukase of 1821 the United States would "contest the right of Russia to any territorial establishment on this continent," and "assume distinctly the principle that the American continents are no longer subjects for *any* new European colonial establishments." A few days later, he instructed Rush on the same subject. After insisting that "the present condition of the north-west coast of this continent" was of manifold importance to the United States, he contended that all treaty recognition of "the exclusive colonial rights of Spain on these continents...has been extinguished by the fact of the independence of the South American nations and of Mexico. Those independent nations will possess the rights incident to that condition, and their territories will, of course, be subject to no *exclusive* right of navigation in their vicinity, or of access to them by any foreign nation. A necessary consequence of this state of things will be that the American continents, henceforth, will no longer be subject to *colonisation.* Occupied by civilised, independent nations, they will be accessible to Europeans, and each other, on that footing alone ; and the Pacific Ocean, in every part of it, will remain open to the navigation of all nations, in like manner with the Atlantic."

Corresponding instructions had been sent to Middleton at the Court of St Petersburg, and in each case the initiative may be attributed to Adams. Though questions of foreign policy were discussed by the Cabinet, and a right of supervision exercised by the President, the instructions to diplomatic agents formed the portion of the labours of the Secretary of State in which he had the freest scope. In the present instance, it may reasonably be assumed that the share of the President in the instructions to Rush and Middleton was confined to an approval of the resistance to all the pretensions of Russia, and a glance through the phrases in which this policy was maintained. Monroe, moreover, was wont to turn to his Ministers for drafts of the paragraphs of his Message which treated of the subjects with which their several departments were concerned. It is not improbable, therefore,—and the recollections of Calhoun support the hypothesis—that Adams

deduced from his peculiar theories of national independence the principle that the future colonisation of
America by Europeans was inadmissible, and saw it
escape the challenge of the Cabinet and of the Russian
Ambassador, both concerned less with generalisations
than with their application to the subjects in dispute.
The assent of the President to the draft despatches
would readily follow.   This gained, the recapitulation
of what had been assumed in the negotiations found its
natural expression in the President's Message, and at
the same time completed for this portion of the United
States policy that manifesto to Russia, Great Britain
and the world in general which Adams so strongly
advocated.   Such a genesis seems the more credible
from the difficulty of the argument against colonisation,
and from its known accordance with the logic of the
Secretary of State.

The Law of Nature, he seems to have believed,
dictated that whenever a body of men in occupation of
a determinable territory desired to rule themselves.
they had an inherent right to carry their desire into
effect.   In the New World, this right had been confirmed by facts; in the Old, it was still defied by the
Holy Alliance.

With the politics of Europe, the United States
had nothing to do.   In whatever touched the western
hemisphere, their rights and interests were concerned.
They themselves had struck a vital blow at the old
system of governing dependencies, and the work was
being completed by the South Americans.   "It was
impossible," he said in conversation, "that the old
exclusive and excluding colonial system should much

longer endure anywhere.... The whole system of modern colonisation was an abuse of government, and it was time that it should come to an end." "If the Holy Allies should subdue America," he told the Cabinet a year later, "the ultimate result of their undertaking would be to recolonise them, partitioned out among themselves." Any revival of the colonial system, then, was an intolerable retrogression. It only remained to prove that it affected the interests of the United States. Having done this, to his own satisfaction, by showing that it would impair the right of free intercourse with all America, he arrived at the dogma that the American continents were henceforth not to be considered as subjects for future colonisation by any European powers.

In determining upon the authorship of the Monroe Doctrine, the argument from personal probability seems to be specially powerful. Which of the two men, it may be asked, was the more likely to formulate new canons of public law? Monroe, with little or "no relish for literature and philosophy," and as President, prone to indecision even on particular questions of action, had reached the evening of life, and the failing health which often attends it. His great wish was for peace, and he looked forward to release from the service of a lifetime. His leisure was to be spent in literary labours which have added little to his fame, and which may perhaps be described as well-meaning but commonplace. Adams, on the other hand, was in the prime both of physical and mental vigour. Student enough to have "the air rather of a scholar than of a statesman," he combined New England powers of abstract thought with a political insight which saved him from being a mere doctrinaire. He was a born individualist, and his social asperity helped him to play the part in international affairs. He possessed rare power of governing his emotions by his reason. Having thought out the separation of American principles from European, his wrath was roused by the slightest invasion of the rights of the Americans, while he could calmly tolerate far more flagrant oppression of Europeans. The key-note of his policy was the perfect equality of America with Europe, and of the United States with the older powers. He proved that the Holy Alliance had no claim to pronounce upon the formation of an American system by pointing to the indisputable fact that its members had not asked America to pronounce upon their European system. The Czar had lectured the United States, and it was "due in candor" that the United States should lecture the Czar.

The occasion and the principles of the Monroe Doctrine, therefore, point to the authorship of Adams. The lack of correspondence between Monroe and the Doctrine which bears his name becomes evident, on the other hand, to those who study both. His biographer, admitting that "as a rule, he was not very skilful with his pen," and that probably he "had but little conception of the lasting effect which his words would produce," is compelled to attribute the force of his dicta to the fact that they express "not only the opinion then prevalent, but a tradition of other days which had gradually been expanded." From external evidence, however, it seems clear that the Monroe Doctrine, if in truth Monroe's, must have been the result of an inspiration which swept away some of his former opinions. In his Message of the previous year, he had expressed strong sympathy with the cause of the Greeks, and in the original drafts in 1823 he had proposed, in effect, to recognise their independence. He had there also strongly censured the invasion of Spain by France, and the principles professed by the king of France in justification. The actual Message, however, insists on the position of the United States as merely "anxious and interested spectators" of European affairs; desiring to see liberty and happiness established there, but disclaiming all idea of interfering save when their own rights were invaded or seriously menaced. The principle on which the allied powers had thought it proper to interpose by force in the internal concerns of Spain is tolerated as "satisfactory to themselves"; and only to be resented by the United States if extended to their own hemisphere. In declaring the policy of the United States "to consider the Government *de facto* as the legitimate Government for us," all idea of assisting the Greeks is tacitly abandoned.

With regard to revolution in the New World also a similar change of tone may be perceived. While every day of actual independence strengthened the claim of the Spanish colonies as against the mother-country, the absolute neutrality of the United States is insisted on more strongly than for years before. In 1818, Adams himself had furnished the paragraph on South America, and next year he had endeavoured to avoid offence to Spain by securing the expurgation of the President's draft. The Message of 1820, however, had drawn a favourable picture of the success of the revolutions, and had inferred "that an adjustment will finally take place on the basis proposed by the colonies." "To promote that result by friendly counsels with other powers, including Spain herself," the President declared to have been "the uniform policy of this Government." Next year, the same sentiments were repeated. In his second inaugural address, Monroe defended the neutral policy of the United States, and predicted the success of the colonies. The December Message announced that it might be presumed, and was earnestly hoped, that the Government of Spain, encouraged by the friendly counsel of the United States, would be so wise and magnanimous as to terminate the exhausting controversy on the basis of colonial independence. In the special Message of March 8th, 1822, which advocated the recognition of the colonies, Monroe did not hesitate to acknowledge the sympathy with which their cause had always been regarded by the United States, and at the close of the year, he repeated his expressions of hope that Spain would soon end the contest. Now, however, the world is informed that it is obvious that she can never subdue the new Governments, and "that it is still the policy of the United States to leave the parties to themselves, in the hope that other powers will pursue the same course."

In respect to the revolutionists of both hemispheres, then, the Monroe Doctrine is not in perfect harmony with the views of the President as previously expressed in public. It coincides, on the other hand, with the consistent teachings of Adams. Its keynote is the sharp political severance of America from Europe. In the mouth of Monroe, who had been wont to sound the praise of liberty in Spain, Portugal and Greece, this rings false. With the strains of Adams it is in perfect accord.

Stratford Canning, the moment he set foot on American soil, had hastened to engage the Secretary of State on the subject of the slave-trade. "Europe and America," he reports Adams as saying in a private conversation, "had each a sphere of its own, in either of whose limits the joint interference of both parties would, in all probability, prove generally useless, and frequently embarrassing. The distance which separates those quarters of the world, and the difference of prevailing opinions in each, appear in his judgment to mark out for the United States a separate and independent course." How these views were impressed upon the Cabinet, has already been described. The political system of the United States, as henceforth to be maintained, was to be essentially republican, and essentially pacific,—"studiously avoiding all involvement in the combinations of European politics, cultivating peace and friendship with the most absolute monarchies." By accepting his policy, Adams claimed, "we avowed republicanism, but we disclaimed propagandism. We asserted national independence...we disavowed all interference with European affairs." Just so far as he desired, the Monroe Doctrine declares the separation of America from Europe.

On its second great principle—the equality between the continents—his opinions had been, if possible, even more strongly pronounced. "This amicable march on parallel lines," he had told Stratford Canning, "might be considered as not only prescribed by Nature, but also as having received the sanction of the European powers; who, in their transactions for the general settlement of affairs, have never recurred to the United States for their assistance or participation." He was always in favour of asserting international individualism —of acting in American matters without reference to the opinion of the Old World. He demanded of the British Minister who questioned the right of the United States to make settlements in a district claimed by Great Britain, "What would be thought in England if Mr Rush were to address the Secretary of State on the occasion of a regiment being destined for New South Wales or the Shetland Islands?" He at first retorted on Alexander by telling his representative that the United States regretted that the Emperor's political principles had not yet led him to the same conclusion with themselves as to the South American question. Early in the following year, he startled the French Minister by declaring that he presumed that France would not interfere between the colonies and Spain without consulting the United States as well as her European Allies. In the Cabinet, he developed and defended the same policy with regard to the Holy Alliance, and the words of the Monroe Doctrine seem to have been the result.

In the third great principle of the Monroe Doctrine, —that the United States possess an interest in everything that touches the Western hemisphere,—Adams had, up to a certain point, been equally consistent. Four years earlier, he had maintained that the world was to be familiarised with " the idea of considering our dominion to be the continent of North America. From the time when we became an independent people, it was as much a law of nature that this should become our pretension as that the Mississippi should flow to the sea." He had really thought, he exclaimed in anger, that the United States were at least to be left unmolested on their continent of North America. "As to an American system," he notes, before Florida had passed into United States hands, "we have it, we constitute the whole of it." Being careful to speak only as a private individual, he had told the British Ambassador, months before the presidential Message of 1823 was thought of, that "the policy of their Government, as well as the course of circumstances, had hitherto excluded the United States from any immediate connection with the general system of European affairs. With respect to the vast continent of the West, the United States must necessarily take a warm and decided interest in whatever determined the fate, or affected the welfare, of its component members." This view of the interests of the Republic in "this hemisphere" or "these continents" is expressed in his instructions to Rush and Middleton, and maintained throughout the course of his propositions to the Cabinet.

During several years, then, Adams had steadily treated the supremacy of the United States on the continent of North America as an established fact, and the progress of events had caused him to declare their interest in the whole of the New World. The Monroe Doctrine, however, though it announces only that they cannot "behold with indifference" the extension of the political system of the Allies to any portion of the

continent, speaks with warmth of those whom it terms
"our southern brethren." In this respect it savours
more of Monroe than of Adams. The latter was no
lover of the South Americans. He saw that the
enthusiasm of his countrymen for the cause of those
who at first sight seemed to be following in their own
footsteps was based on unsubstantial sentiment. His
disagreement with their conclusions was embittered by
the fact that Clay, at this time one of his great political
rivals, was the champion of the insurgents. Hence he
sneers at fanatics and idols alike. "Although we
have done more than any other nation for the South
Americans," he had discovered early in 1820, "they
are discontented because we have not espoused their
cause in arms. With empty professions of friendship,
they have no real sympathy with us." Vague offers of
commercial advantages in the future, coupled with
prayers for secret favours in the present, had compelled
him to "distrust these South American gentlemen."
The President's expressions of sympathy for them
approached, in his view, to breaches of neutrality. He
had little expectation, he informed Clay, of any beneficial result to the United States from connection,
political or commercial, with the South. There was no
community of principles between them. Dislike of
individuals, however, was no reason for political opposition to their cause. The object attributed by Calhoun
to the Monroe Doctrine, "to countenance and encourage
these young republics as far as we could with propriety,"
was the object also of Adams. While denying their
claim to kinship, he agreed with the Monroe Doctrine
in asserting their right to independence. The opinions

that Spain could not hope to subdue the colonies, that the United States should continue to observe perfect neutrality, and that nothing should be actually risked for the sake of South America, are likewise common to both.   A single phrase, inserted perhaps by the President, or adopted by Adams as a harmless concession to the views of his colleagues, cannot of itself disprove his authorship.

There is reason, then, for regarding it as improbable that Monroe either could or would have evolved the Doctrine which bears his name.   There is equal reason for affirming that, with the exception of the expression of affection for the South, the Doctrine states exactly the principles of Adams.   His own account of the transactions which preceded it shows that he desired to announce those principles to the world, that he embodied them in a document for the President's inspection, and that the President substituted for the original draft " paragraphs respecting the Greeks, Spain, Portugal and South America " which seemed to him " quite unexceptionable."   The logical conclusion seems to be that the conception of the Monroe Doctrine and much of its phraseology came from Adams, and that the share of Monroe did not extend beyond revision.

This hypothesis receives some support from the scanty evidence of contemporaries.   Clay recognised in the words of the President the work of several hands; and Adams, by creed and habit an egoist, notes his opinion that " the part relating to foreign affairs was the best part of the Message."   William Plumer, a Congressman from New Hampshire, whose vote for Adams had been the only one cast against the reelection of Monroe, and who was about this time a constant visitor at the Department of State, asserts in his diary for 1824 that it was only the firmness of the Secretary of State that determined the President to retain the paragraphs relating to the interference of the Holy Alliance with Spanish America. A negative argument may also be of value. Adams himself, in his Eulogy on the Life and Character of James Monroe, discusses specifically the public acts which had been indisputably those of the deceased statesman. The evidence of Addington has made it clear that in 1823 the Secretary did not dissent from the President's view of the diplomacy then proceeding as "the most delicate and important measure of his whole administration." In 1831, however, the only allusion to the Monroe Doctrine is a rhetorical flourish, praising the late President for "controlling by a firm though peaceful policy the hostile spirit of the European alliance against republican South America."

Coming from Adams, the Doctrine was a master-stroke, worthy of one who, according to a veteran diplomatist, knew the politics of all Europe. Great Britain could not but applaud the declaration of a policy which she had herself suggested. At the same time she lost the glory of its initiation, while the people of the United States were flattered by the appearance of leadership. This gain, moreover, was effected without loss in the force of the blow. The United States and Great Britain severally declaring a similar policy were no less formidable than Great Britain associating the United States with herself in a public manifesto. At no cost to themselves, the

United States had received from Great Britain an acknowledgment of their eminence in the New World, and a demonstration of their right to take a principal part in whatever arrangements were imposed upon South America. Europe was handled with equal skill. While tolerating the principles of France so far as they affected the Old World, the Message checkmated her designs on Spanish America. Adams's insight into the political situation had never allowed him to share in the prevailing dread of the Holy Alliance. The Doctrine, however, quieted the apprehensions of the public, and, at little risk, gained for the United States the credit of international fearlessness. Spain, on the other hand, being harmless, was treated more gently than before. It is in dealing with the Spanish Americans, however, that the Message appears cleverest. By speaking of interference with them as " the manifestation of an unfriendly disposition towards the United States," which it was impossible for the latter to " behold with indifference," the new republics were invited to believe that they had gained a protector. The words, on the other hand, apart from their spirit, did not absolutely commit the Executive, and the Executive had the Constitution in reserve. At small expense, therefore, the Monroe Doctrine had foiled Europe and delighted America.

From a personal point of view, Adams might regard it with equal satisfaction. Many months earlier, it had become evident that all public measures were likely to be affected by the struggle for the Presidency which would be determined in 1824. The Secretary of State, by his own confession, felt that if he were not elected, it would be the equivalent of a vote of censure on his conduct in office. Every successor to Washington had been either Vice-president or Secretary of State, and the Vice-presidents were no longer competitors. True to his sense of duty, he would do nothing to secure the prize, but the strongest convictions could not require him to damage his own prospects, or to obscure his rightful claims. He had begged Monroe not to irritate the Holy Alliance, but to hand over the Administration to his successor in peace. His ideal of policy was "to make up an American cause and adhere inflexibly to that," and to embody it in a declaration which might serve as a scheme of policy for the future. In the Monroe doctrine his ends were achieved, and at the same time that he outbade Great Britain, he had the satisfaction of outbidding Clay. The policy, though statesmanlike, was popular; and in the verdict of the people on the Administration its author was deeply concerned.

CHAPTER VI.

The Reception of the Monroe Doctrine.

Of the statecraft that attended the birth of the Monroe Doctrine the citizens of the United States saw little or nothing. Congress itself, like the British Parliament, was ignorant of the communications between Canning and Rush. What appeared was that the Holy Alliance had threatened the liberties of America, and that Monroe had come forward as their champion. At the same time, he had voiced the spirit of the nation, elated with forty years of unprecedented progress. It was only natural, therefore, that men should rally to the Administration with one accord. Addington was impressed by the perfect unanimity with which the whole republic echoed " the explicit and manly tone with which the President has treated the subject of European interference in the affairs of this hemisphere with a view to the re-subjugation of those territories which have emancipated themselves from European domination." The flame of enthusiasm melted all reserve. The seeming divergence of the new policy from Monroe's habitual caution, and the apparent assumption by the Executive of the right to determine the course of the United States, passed unnoticed. Even that part of the Doctrine which dealt with colonisation was hardly remarked. Addington says not a word about it, and the *National Intelligencer* and the provincial press treat it with equal silence.

In fastening thus upon what was construed as the determination of the United States to resist hostile interference with the new republics, the people found a twofold gratification. Their fears were banished by the firm attitude of the Executive. At the same time they felt that, as Monroe's friends could assure him, the Message would be esteemed to have given to their national character new claims upon the civilised world. Whether Democrats or Federalists, all were sincere republicans, and all were proud that the Republic should have bearded the monarchs who had bidden it apologise for its very existence. Europe, they felt, must respect, if it did not love them. The spirit of nationality, therefore, was roused, and in conjunction with the visit of Lafayette, made the year 1824 remarkable for a general military mania.

While the Administration gained fresh lustre, feeling ran high in favour of Great Britain. Outside the Cabinet, no one dreamed that the Monroe Doctrine could give her anything but satisfaction. The press and society alike, according to her representative at Washington, called for union with her to preserve the liberties of the Western hemisphere. The Administration, whatever the sentiments of its members, took some steps in the same direction. The words in which the Secretary of State strove to impress Addington with a sense of his goodwill have already been quoted.

Six months after the communication of the Message, when the rage of the people against the Holy Alliance was becoming less fevered, the President publicly remarked that the policy of the two countries was essentially the same, and that his personal knowledge of some of the chief members of the English Cabinet gave him entire confidence in their judgment and integrity.

With the American people, moreover, the Monroe Doctrine lost nothing in esteem through its vagueness. Three weeks after its delivery, indeed, the House of Representatives requested the President to communicate, if possible, information relative to the threatened interference of European powers in the affairs of South America. "I have to state," he replied, "that I possess no information on that subject, not known to Congress, which can be disclosed without injury to the public good." The House accepted the refusal, and proceeded to endorse the principles of the Administration, in so far as they related to non-interference with Europe. It was felt that by a motion of Webster's, then before the House, in favour of sending a commissioner to Greece, "Europe and America were injudiciously blended together"; and although the flame of universal liberty burnt high, a general expression of sympathy with the Greeks was carried in its place. The voice of the Administration, it was clear, was the voice of Congress and of the people.

In Great Britain also, public opinion approved the Message. From sentiment or from interest, many were enthusiastic in the cause of the revolted colonies, and none could fail to see that the Monroe Doctrine told in their favour. The Opposition, at least, regarded the South American question as solved; and a rise in the price of Spanish-American securities showed that the commercial world did not ignore the policy of the United States. Ministers, too, had the satisfaction of seeing the United States take a course which they themselves had suggested. Canning has even been regarded as the author of a Doctrine which might not have been enunciated without the impulse of his proposals. While insisting that his communications to Rush had constituted a *sounding*, not an overture, he frankly acknowledged that the President had materially helped the British Government. The Message, it was evident, had come opportunely to assist Great Britain in repelling the invitation urged upon her from all quarters of the Continent to take part in the proposed conference on the affairs of Spanish-America. Spain, it was true, had not directly included her among the powers to which she had appealed, but Ofalia spared no effort to induce her to delay the recognition which, he hoped, this congress would avert. France, Austria and Russia argued unceasingly that their views were the same as her own, and that by frowning upon the conference, she would be simply delaying the restoration of order which all desired. Canning, however, held firmly to the views expressed in his conference with Polignac, and the arrival of the Monroe Message gave him the moral support of the United States. The Congress, he informed A'Court, had been broken in all its limbs before, and the speech of the President had given it the *coup de grace*. Though Chateaubriand might laugh at the naval strength of the United States, his congress would have been an attempt of the nations which had little power or interest in South America to settle its affairs against the will of those which had much. By itself, it is true, the Monroe Doctrine might have done little to check the Allies. The mere declaration by the United States of their attitude towards any European power which should interpose for the purpose of controlling the destiny of the new republics did not deter the powers from continuing to urge Great Britain to take part in a conference with this end in view. It was of great use, however, in strengthening the hands of Canning. The refusal of Great Britain became conclusive, and the despatch to A'Court at the end of January put an end to the project.

So unexpected and so opportune, indeed, was the declaration, that the powers of Europe and the English Opposition inferred that it had been made in consequence of communications from Great Britain. This must have made Canning's failure to win over Rush more unpalatable than before. He claimed credit, it is true, for the actual share which he had taken in inspiring a measure on the whole advantageous to Great Britain. But he could not be blind to the triumph of "that scoundrel Adams" in thus taking the reins out of his hands, and in trumpeting the praises of republicanism in the face of the British monarchy. In refuting diplomatically the suggestion of Chateaubriand that Great Britain had dictated the Monroe Doctrine, therefore, he insists on every point of difference between the South American policy of the two nations. The one, he says, has recognised the independence of the colonies, the other has not. The declaration of Monroe may be interpreted as condemning the interference of Spain herself with Spanish-America. This, says Canning, would constitute "as important a difference between his view of the subject and ours, as perhaps it is possible to conceive."

While thus able to qualify, though slightly, the agreement of Great Britain with the second portion of the Monroe Doctrine, he fell with the more vigour upon the first. Twenty-five years later, Calhoun denounced this portion of the Message as inaccurate, since the continents as a whole had not assumed and maintained a free and independent condition, and as also improper, since the United States were professing to act in concert with Great Britain. British statesmen, it was clear, could not share the calm conviction of Adams that their colonies must fall naturally into the lap of the United States. On the 2nd January, Rush was made to feel the difference between natural law and common sense. The Secretary of State had formulated, and the President had announced, the principle that no future European colonisation could be permitted in continents of whose geographical limits they themselves were ignorant. "Suppose," argued the British Foreign Secretary, " that any new British expedition were to end in the discovery of land proximate to either part of the American continent, North or South, would the United States object to Great Britain planting a colony there?" The question, it may be presumed, was unanswerable. Canning followed it by rejecting the idea of a triple negotiation at St Petersburg for the settlement of the north-west boundary question. The reason, he admitted, was the President's edict commanding the cessation throughout " the continents of America" of a susceptibility of being colonised from Europe. Great Britain could not, he maintained, "acknowledge the right of any power to proclaim such a principle, much less to bind other countries to the observance of it. If we were to be repelled from the shores of America, it would not matter to us whether that repulsion were effected by the Ukase of Russia excluding us from the sea; or by the new Doctrine of the President prohibiting us from the land. But we cannot yield obedience to either." At the same time he was careful to inform the French Government of his inability to understand the President's prohibition. His instructions to the British commissioners, five months later, were equally explicit. Describing the declaration of the President as " very extraordinary," he announced that " the principle was one which His Majesty's Ministers were prepared to combat in the most unequivocal manner, maintaining that whatever right of colonising the unappropriated portions of America has been hitherto enjoyed by Great Britain in common with the other powers of Europe may still be exercised in perfect freedom, without affording the slightest cause of umbrage to the United States."

In France, where the presidential Message attracted much attention, both parts of the Doctrine were condemned alike. At a dinner at Prince Polignac's, Rush complained that in upholding the principle of non-colonisation he had to face the whole British Cabinet with the probable influence of Russia superadded. He only learned, however, that the weight of France was likely to be thrown into the same scale. The men of

Brazil and Chili heard with unprecedented rapidity that the extreme Royalists could not contain their indignation, and that the Russian Ambassador in Paris, who had boasted that in any event the Czar could keep North America neutral, was thunderstruck by the declaration of Monroe. Ministers and people saw Canning behind the scenes. The British Ambassador could not at first succeed, even by pressing chronology into the service, in convincing Chateaubriand that the Doctrines were not set forth in virtue of an understanding with Great Britain. " A declaration of the principles," urged the Minister for Foreign Affairs, " upon which the President affects to pronounce that the New World shall in future be governed, made at a time when the American Government is wholly unable to enforce such pretensions, ought to be resisted by all the powers possessing either territory or commercial interests in that hemisphere." A week later, the British Ambassador forced him to disclaim his suspicions by reading the explanatory despatch of Canning. The suggestion that the prohibition of future colonisation on the continents of America had been brought forward by the President to meet " the unwarrantable pretensions " of the Russian Ukase, he accepted as satisfactory. The sole official inference which France professed to draw from the Monroe Doctrine, therefore, was that it would be improper to invite the United States to the conference on South America.

The other members of the Holy Alliance came to the same conclusion. Metternich, admitting that the Message was in exact conformity with the republican principles avowed and constantly acted upon by the Government of the United States, prophesied once more the calamities which the New World would bring upon the Old. The Czar was at this time ill, and the labours of his ministers were divided between urging Great Britain to attend the proposed conference at Paris, and upholding the Russian claims to the north-west territory of America. In Prussia, the Message gave great offence; but the attitude of the court on the Spanish-American question was described by the British Ambassador as passive. The newly-established commercial relations with Spanish-America were cherished, and the only retaliation deemed expedient was a slight delay in filling the place vacated by the death of the Prussian Minister at Washington.

The United States, Great Britain, France, and the remaining members of the Holy Alliance, then, received the Message with keen interest. Even the smaller powers of Europe showed themselves alive to its importance. The official Gazette of Lisbon described the cordial relations between Great Britain and the United States, and the satisfaction with which the former regarded the opposition to the pretensions of Russia. The king of the Netherlands pointed out to the British Ambassador the danger lest a trans-Atlantic confederation should be formed under the influence and protection of the northern republic. Spain alone, where the king listened only to what pleased him, while "the infatuated adherence of His Catholic Majesty's advisers to the errors of all their predecessors without exception" alienated the most Bourbon of foreign statesmen, pursued her course without the slightest sign of attention.

The immediate political influence of the Monroe Doctrine on America south of the United States, it is almost impossible to estimate. The people, if they noticed the presidential Message at all, would read, weeks or months after its delivery, a transcript of some European journal which discussed it, or would hear a rumour that the head of a nation which they could not appreciate had pronounced in their favour against an enemy whose power they could not measure. The declaration, it is safe to say, aroused among the mass of their "southern brethren" no wave of affection for the people of the United States. The rulers of Spanish-America, however, must have been better informed both as to the words of the President and their value. A month after the opening of Congress, the Columbian diplomatists at Washington appeared to the British Minister "to entertain much appre-hension of the threatened interference of the European powers in the affairs of their country," and to "evidently look to Great Britain as the main anchor on which they rest their hopes for the prevention of that inter-ference." Measured by Spanish standards of expression, indeed, the words of the President seem but lukewarm, and though the officials of South America made the most of them, they were not the equivalent of Bolivar's foreign legion. In April 1824, the Vice-president of Columbia opened the Assembly by describing the Monroe Doctrine as "an act eminently just and worthy of the classic land of liberty—a policy consolatory to human nature." He informed the people, however, that the Executive was sedulously occupied in reducing the question to decisive and conclusive points.

The President of Buenos Ayres, likewise, placed in the forefront of his message a statement of relations with the United States. Significantly enough, he ignored the second portion of the Monroe Doctrine altogether. The Minister to Washington, he said, had been instructed to inform the Government of the approbation with which Buenos Ayres regarded "the two great principles of the abolition of privateering and of the cessation of European colonisation in the territory of America." The representative of Brazil, even in the first flush of gratitude for recognition, suggested that action was expedient.

Mexico alone showed a disposition to over-estimate the immediate political effect of the Doctrine. The language in which the President congratulates his fellow-citizens on their recognition by the United States, is not, indeed, as glowing as that in which he describes how Britain interposed her trident to save them from the Holy Alliance. Benefits, however, though secondary ones, were anticipated from the United States, and the disappointment was acute enough to provoke the charge of ill-faith. By the Message of May 1826, the Mexican Congress was informed that "the memorable promise of President Monroe is not sustained by the present Government of the United States of the North, and the compact made on this subject has been broken."

In general, therefore, if it be possible to generalise from such materials, it would seem that the Governments of South America were grateful for the Monroe

Doctrine as an expression of sympathy with their cause. They could not, however, perceive that it removed their difficulties. They did not view it as profoundly affecting either their international status or their prospects. What they desired was specific agreement to promote the objects which the Doctrine had in view. For this end, among others, they had for some time been striving to bring about a general Congress at Panama. The Monroe Message was followed by an invitation to the United States to attend it.

CHAPTER VII.

THE RELATION OF THE MONROE DOCTRINE TO INTERNATIONAL LAW.

THUS far the Monroe Doctrine has been treated from a historical or political point of view. The general aspect of affairs which preceded it has been sketched, and more minute attention devoted to the negotiations and discussions from which it directly emerged. An attempt has been made to determine its authorship, and to indicate its immediate political effects upon both America and Europe. The Doctrine has commonly been credited, however, with an authority greater than that which its history or reputed parentage could bestow. In defiance of the opinion of American publicists, many of the citizens of the United States have regarded it as a part of International Law—the body of rules prevailing between States. To violate its principles, therefore, has been to attack not only interests, but also rights. Hence it has been involved in fresh confusion. Its interpretation—its very nature —have never been placed beyond dispute. A keen English observer of trans-Atlantic institutions has termed it a fixed and permanent state of American opinion. The grandson and literary executor of Monroe has explained it as meaning that the People were the originators and supporters of all governments, and the sovereigns in the exercise of the powers of government. To German thinkers, it has seemed a law laid down by America for Europe, and by the United States for their neighbours. At every stage of its history, in fact, new translations have been added. The claim that an act 'violates the Monroe Doctrine,' therefore, cannot readily be refuted; and the alleged violation is regarded as synonymous with a breach of International Law. Both points are open to dispute, and the confusion may extend both to International Law and international relations. Such a stream of error can only be checked at its source. If the Monroe Doctrine did not become by enunciation a part of the body of rules prevailing between the States, it is clear that repetition by the power which enunciated it cannot force it into the international code. To estimate its legal value, as well as to understand its specific meaning, it must be examined line by line.

The declaration of Monroe with regard to colonisation has been defined as a foreclosure of the whole continent against all future European dominion, however derived. Standing alone, it is inexplicable. An eminent commentator on the writings of the chief publicist of the United States has maintained that the question was one of political geography. Applying to the condition of the continents a recognised principle of public law, Monroe, he explains, laid down that in fact the whole of them was within the territory of some responsible state.   Hence they were not *ferae naturae* and open to appropriation.   A recent American writer, on the other hand, in discussing the corresponding instructions to Rush, contends that "if Mr Adams intended to...announce that territory already occupied by civilised powers was not subject to future colonisation, he merely stated a truism.   But in its application to the American continents at that time, the announcement was far from being a truism."   The truth was that the United States were one among four chief powers dominant on the continent of North America, while south of Mexico they had no possessions whatever.   The northern continent, at least, was not fully explored.   Up to the time of this declaration, any portion of it to the northward, exclusive of the districts claimed by Russia, Great Britain and the United States, had been a legitimate subject for colonisation by any civilised state.   Could any single power, then, claim the sanction of international law for the principle that this part of the American continent was no longer subject to the colonisation of others?   The answer is a simple statement of the law of occupation as it existed in 1823. Every civilised state, then as now, had the right of extending its dominions by fresh appropriations of land, so long as it refrained from encroaching on the dominions of another.   The rest, however, since their own opportunities for extension were diminished, might demand that the appropriation should be real.   No Bull or Ukase could of itself give valid title.   The claim must have been preceded by the discovery of the lands in question—discovery implying the definite visit of a commissioned person—and by some overt act of

annexation to the state. Though the ultimate test of
sovereignty would be government, such official discovery
and annexation would suffice, for the time being, to
secure the territory against appropriation by friendly
powers. The declaration of Monroe, however, com-
prised two continents. It applied, therefore, in part
to territory discovered and claimed by Great Britain
and Russia; in part, to territory presumed to be in
the possession of insurgents whom the United States
alone had recognised as independent; and in part, to
any additional territory which the progress of exploration
might reveal. In the view of public law, then, it was
worthless. The United States could not by a declaration
affect the international status of lands claimed, ruled,
or discovered by other powers. They might proclaim
in advance the policy which they would adopt when
such questions should arise, but no unilateral act could
change the Law of Nations.

The explanations furnished by Adams himself invested the Doctrine with no juridical value. His
instructions to Rush were embodied in the protocol of
the 20th conference between the British and American
commissioners of 1824. The principle that no part of
the American continent is henceforward to be open to
colonisation from Europe was there defended on the
grounds "that the independence of the late Spanish
provinces precluded any new settlement within the
limits of their respective jurisdictions; that the United
States claimed the exclusive right of sovereignty of all
the territory within the parallels of latitude which
include as well the mouth of the Columbia as the
heads of that river and of all its tributary streams;

and that with respect to the whole of the remainder of that continent not naturally occupied, the powers of Europe were debarred from making new settlements by the claim of the United States as derived under their title from Spain."

An adequate explanation of the principle thus formulated, and of the manner in which the rights and interests of the United States were involved in it, can only be found in the political views of Adams. Holding as he did that the Union must soon include all North America, that the Colonial System was doomed, and that the continent was accessible to Europeans and to the civilised nations occupying it only on the footing of national independence, he might if he thought fit direct his diplomatic subordinates to assume that such views were incontestable. In so doing, however, he quoted postulates of his own; not portions of the body of rules prevailing between states. The Law of Nations could be changed only by the renunciation, made tacitly or expressly by every civilised power, of its right to colonise any unoccupied part of the western hemisphere. In the words of an American jurist of repute, " the principle,...if intended to prevent Russia from stretching her borders on the Pacific further to the south, went far beyond any limit of interference that had hitherto been set up. What right had the United States to control Russia in gaining territory on the Pacific, or planting colonies there, when they themselves had neither territory nor colony to be endangered within thousands of miles?" The protest of the powers that believed their interests to be most affected showed that the declaration against

European colonisation was in no way International Law.

The second portion of the Monroe Doctrine has been variously treated by publicists. Some have cited it as an example of intervention; others, as an illustration of the principle of non-intervention. Wheaton, Blunt-schli, Andrés Bello, Travers Twiss, and Heffter may be instanced as representing a cosmopolitan body of specialists who, by ignoring the doctrine in their general treatises, tacitly deny its claim to be numbered among the laws of nations. Such a claim, indeed, must be founded on the belief that Monroe, like Jefferson in discussing the duties of neutrals in 1793, laid down principles based on reason and confirmed by practice. A declaration of opinion or of policy, however valuable to the family of nations, could not, save by their own adoption, affect their code. The words of the Message themselves, none the less, bear out the story of its construction as a formulation of political principle. The attitude assumed by the United States as benevolent spectators of the internal relations of Europe is in the opening sentences founded on policy and not on law. Their position in defending their own rights, and in taking a more active part in the affairs of their own hemisphere, is next defined as the converse of the first. It is nowhere suggested that their duty compels them to be passive in Europe and active in America. Similarly the succeeding paragraph does not allege it as a breach of law that " the political system of the allied powers is essentially different in this respect from that of America." It is hinted, however, that the difference which exists in their respective governments would impel the states of the Old World to interfere in the New. They are informed, therefore, that the whole nation is devoted to its own form of government. "We should," says the President, " consider any attempt on their part to extend their system to any portion of this hemisphere as dangerous to our peace and safety." In this definition of the eventual opinions of the United States, there is no suggestion of a law. The words, at first sight inconclusive, admit of the explanation that any action against the new republics, if based on the principle of Legitimacy, would by implication condemn the United States, and cause them to fear that they themselves would be the next to suffer. Further commentary is supplied by what follows. With the existing American colonies of Europe, the United States will not interfere. " But with the Governments who have declared their independence and maintained it, and whose independence we have, on great consideration and on just principles, acknowledged, we could not view any interposition for the purpose of oppressing them, or controlling in any other manner their destiny, by any European power, in any other light than as the manifestation of an unfriendly disposition towards the United States." This is the kernel of the Doctrine. Its very obscurity suggests that it is not part of 'the rough jurisprudence of nations.' Its spirit, indeed, seems rather to transcend the bounds of law. Recognition of independence, as all admit, should be the mere acknowledgment of an indisputable fact. The United States, however, seem to claim that by recognising Spanish America they have identified its interests

with their own. "The essence of intervention," it is
true "is illegality"; and the United States, like
England in 1826, might profitably declare their intention of opposing it in certain specified cases. Such
a declaration as this, however, though perhaps justifiable
by legal principles, belongs to policy, and not to law.
It could not be held to bind the United States to
interfere in the cases which they had indicated, nor
could it justify them in interfering if any of those
cases should be proved inconsistent with the Law of
Nations. From a legal point of view, therefore, it has
as little value as the paragraph which follows, and
which declares that the United States will preserve
their neutrality in the war between the new governments and Spain, unless in the interests of their
security it becomes indispensable for them to abandon it.

The remainder of the Monroe Doctrine seems to
repeat in other words the declarations which have gone
before. The interest of the United States in the
principles on which the Allies have interposed in Spain
is more explicitly asserted, and their policy of non-
interference with Europe more tersely expressed.
"But in regard to these continents," it is reiterated,
"circumstances are eminently and conspicuously different. It is impossible that the allied powers should
extend their political system to any portion of either
continent without endangering our peace and happiness;
nor can anyone believe that our southern brethren, if
left to themselves, would adopt it of their own accord.
It is equally impossible, therefore, that we should
behold such interposition, in any form, with indifference." The United States, in short, declare that they

will take cognisance of action which endangers their peace and happiness. In so doing, they will be exercising a right which no power can contest. They do not, however, bind themselves, or declare themselves legally bound, to follow any given course as the result of such cognisance. Nor do they define the 'political system' of the Allies. If the latter endeavoured to conquer the new Republics, for Spain or for themselves, without just cause of war, the United States would need no Monroe Doctrine to justify them in stepping in. If, on the other hand, their belief as to the desires of their southern brethren proved erroneous, and the extension of the political system were effected by diplomatic means, or in consequence of appeals to reason, the United States could not derive from the Monroe Doctrine any right to interfere by force. They might meet diplomacy by diplomacy, and reason by reason, but the allegation that their political peace or sentimental happiness was disturbed by the sight of a monarch on the throne of Mexico, or by the accession of Columbia to the Holy Alliance, could not warrant them in a resort to arms. Such action, indeed, would be an intervention against ideas, and parallel to the invasion of Naples by Austria, or of Spain by France. In insisting upon the right of every people to choose its own form of government without external interference, also, the declaration is affirming, but not creating, the Law of Nations. The kernel of this part of the Monroe Doctrine, then, in its second form as in its first, is a vague declaration of policy, and in no way a formulation of rules prevailing between states. The concluding paragraph, predicting the success of the colonies, and once more insisting on neutrality as " still the true policy of the United States," expresses the hope, and not the assurance based on law, that " other powers will pursue the same course."

No line or paragraph of the Monroe Doctrine, therefore, represents an addition to the body of rules prevailing between states. From the first word to the last, it is a declaration of the policy of a single power. To derive from the whole principles which are essentially absent from all the parts, would be contrary to reason. The spirit which breathes through the Message, none the less, seems to threaten a revolution in the Law of Nations. North Americans at this time loved to contrast the *liberty* which was the fundamental principle of the New World, with the *allegiance* which fettered the Old, and to insist upon the severance of the two. Canning appreciated their desires, and expressed his longing to "prevent the drawing of the line of demarcation which I most dread—America versus Europe." In the antithesis between " these continents " and Europe, five times insisted on, lurks the germ of a principle that instead of one family of nations there should be two. It recalls the idea of Jefferson of " a meridian of partition through the ocean which separates the two hemispheres, on the hither side of which no European gun shall ever be heard, nor an American on the other." Carried to its logical conclusion, however the conception of a separate law for America would split the planet into halves. The assertion on the part of the United States of a right to secede from the family of nations must have been met as they themselves met a similar claim at home. The obligations of International Law, it would have been shown, are imposed upon a member of that family at its birth, and are not contracted into at will. Common interests must give rise to international disputes, and disputes postulate at least the possibility of war. To deny an appeal to force in the last resort, therefore, is to shut the door to friendly intercourse. By the admission that Spain has the right to continue her war, by the fervid expression of sympathy with the Greeks, and by the declaration that no interference with the existing colonies or dependencies of any European power is contemplated, the idea of the severance of the hemispheres is, however, for the time being disclaimed. It has been insisted upon in this place because its corollary that the United States are in some way free to lay down the law of nations for America is perhaps the second great source of error with regard to the Monroe Doctrine. That the Doctrine itself is part of International Law, is the first.

CHAPTER VIII.

THE MONROE DOCTRINE AS INTERPRETED BY ITS AUTHOR.

A COMPLETE chapter in the biography of the Monroe Doctrine extends from its enunciation to the close of the Presidency of Adams in 1829. During these five years, the policy of the United States was shaped by the sponsors of the Message of 1823. Their words and conduct, therefore, may be expected to explain and illustrate the principles of policy which it had declared.

The prohibition of future European colonisation led at once to a deadlock with England. The commissioners of 1824 to whom Rush tendered his explanation, together with the proposal to prolong for another decade the temporising convention of 1818, scouted explanation and proposal alike. Neither side could give way, and for nearly a quarter of a century the northwestern boundary question remained unsettled. At the close of the year, the House of Representatives passed a bill for carrying into effect the President's recommendation of a settlement at the mouth of the

Columbia. Addington, fettered by the instructions to Stratford Canning, could only "use every unostensible effort" to procure its rejection by the Senate. In March it was thrown out by a substantial majority, its chief opponent urging that it contravened the claims of Great Britain.

A convention with Russia had for the time being constituted latitude 54·40 the dividing line. No European colonisation being attempted, there was no need for the United States to put their declared principles of policy into practice. Public attention, therefore, centred on that part of the Doctrine which condemned extension to the New World of the political system of the Old. In January Clay proposed that Congress should declare by resolution "that the people of the United States would not see, without serious inquietude, any forcible interposition by the allied powers of Europe" in the quarrel between Spain and the new republics. Four months later, however, he withdrew his motion, on the ground that recent evidence showed that any intention of such interference had been relinquished. Resolutions of the Legislatures of several states approving the action of the President were simply laid on the table.

Meanwhile the question of the recognition of Brazil had thrown fresh light on the meaning of the Message. In the Cabinet Wirt had questioned the expediency of receiving a diplomatic representative from a Government which, though American and revolutionary, was not republican. Calhoun, however, with the support of Adams, warmly opposed any such intervention in the internal government of a foreign nation, and his interpretation of the principles of the United States prevailed. Delayed only for further information as to the fitness of Brazil to be acknowledged as independent, on May 26th, 1824, the recognition was consummated. The Brazilian *charge d'affaires*, however, made his official reception the occasion for suggesting the expediency of translating principle into action. With expressions of gratitude on his lips, he glanced at "the concert of American powers to sustain the general system of American independence. To this," says Adams, "the President did not particularly allude in his answer."

Early in July the Diary, reduced to mere jottings in the ferment of the struggle for the Presidency, outlines a more specific case of appeal to the Monroe Doctrine. The diplomatic representative of Columbia, it appears, had come to Adams with the news that Chasserioux, a former Columbian captain who had entered the service of France, was going to Bogota; that France had offered to recognise Columbia if she would establish monarchy, even that of the house of Bolivar; and that the offer had proved unacceptable. What action, he asked, were the United States prepared to take? The Secretary of State had, as usual, requested a statement in writing; and the reply was determined by a Cabinet consisting of himself, the President and Calhoun. The notes of the decision are a commentary on the Monroe Doctrine. The Columbian Republic, it was resolved, must maintain its own independence, but the United States hoped that France and the Holy Allies would not resort to force against it. Should they be disappointed, their resistance must be determined by Congress. "The movements of the Executive will be as heretofore expressed."

At the same moment the veil of secrecy which had concealed the negotiation between Canning and Rush had in part been lifted. A confidential Message sent by the President to the Senate had been published, and the world could read that "the whole system of South American concerns, connected with a general recognition of South American independence, may again, from hour to hour, become, as it has already been, an object of concerted operation of the highest interest to both nations and to the peace of the world."

At the end of the year Monroe repeated and explained the principles of the Doctrine which wears his name. Spain as a power, he stated, was barely perceptible in her wars with the nations of the South. The United States, in spite of the deep interest which they took "in their independence...and in their enjoyment of all the rights incident thereto, especially in the very important one of instituting their own governments," would not violate these rights by any interference. Of the vibrations of the European balance of power, also, they remained benevolent spectators. "But in regard to our neighbours," he maintained, "the situation is different. It is impossible for the European Governments to interfere in their concerns, especially in those alluded to, which are vital, without affecting us; indeed, the motive which might induce such interference in the present state of the war between the parties, if a war it may be called, is equally applicable to us." In these principles, he is glad to note, some of the powers of Europe have

appeared to acquiesce.   The Message takes its wonted
cognisance of European affairs, and in no way indicates
an advance on that of last year towards the severance
of the two hemispheres.

Two months later the long internal struggle came
to an end.   To the disgust of Jackson and his party,
Clay conferred the Presidency upon Adams, and himself received the office of Secretary of State.   Deeming
him more anxious than his predecessor with respect to
the fate of the new republics, Addington took an early
opportunity of ascertaining his views.   These were
what might have been looked for from the sanguine
champion of South American independence.   Where
Adams had been passive and cautious, Clay " owned
that the object nearest his heart was the definitive
pacification and settlement of the American states."
Above all, he desired the arrangement of a general
association for resisting foreign aggression.   With
Addington's assent, moreover, he invited Great Britain
to join the United States in pressing each of the
remaining Great Powers to admit the principle of
recognition.   All might then, he hoped, unite in urging
Spain to do the same.   He had already sent instructions to the ambassadors at Paris and St Petersburg
to work for such an end.   The Ministers accredited to
the American republics were "to neglect no opportunity
of inculcating on the minds of the rulers of those
states the necessity of infusing temper and moderation
into their proceedings and feelings with regard to
Spain," and to incline them to sacrifice national pride
for the sake of peace with Europe.   The new Secretary
of State, it was clear, did not aim at severing America

from Europe, or at subjugating the South to the North. Declaring himself quite in love with Canning, he hoped to join him in guaranteeing the independence of Cuba, and would even look with equanimity on its junction with the Columbian or Mexican Federation.

It is unnecessary to point out how ill such views as these accorded with the deductions of Adams. Clay was always the apostle of compromise, and Adams found compromise unintelligible. Both agreed, however, in endorsing the Monroe Doctrine. In the same month of May, 1825, Clay instructed Poinsett that the United States could not allow the enterprise and commerce of all Americans to be arbitrarily limited and circumscribed by fresh colonisation on the part of distant foreign powers. "Europe," he maintained, "would be indignant at an attempt to plant a colony on any part of her shores; and her justice must perceive, in the rule contended for, only perfect reciprocity."

In November circumstances arose which kept the whole of the Doctrine for six months in the forefront of politics. At the instigation of Columbia a general congress of Spanish-American States had for years been debated and desired. A meeting at Panama had at last been arranged for the following spring, and the presence of deputies from the United States was requested. Early in November, Columbia, Mexico and Central America sent invitations to the Department of State, mentioning among the subjects of discussion "the manner in which all colonisation of European powers on the American continent shall be resisted, and their interference in the present contest between Spain and her former colonies prevented." Even the

formation of a continental system for the New World
was hinted, and a general desire shown to join with
the United States in putting the Monroe Doctrine into
practice. Clay replied that his government could not
share in or discuss the war with Spain, and suggested
that the topics of the conferences should be defined.
Though the answers were not considered sufficiently
precise, Adams declared in his opening Message to
Congress that the invitation to send Ministers to
Panama had been accepted. In the terms of commercial treaties with South America he had striven for
"the effectual emancipation of the American hemisphere from the thraldom of colonising monopolies and
exclusions," and at the end of December he explained
his wishes in a confidential Message to the Senate.
The Congress at Panama, he suggested, might discuss
an agreement that each of the powers represented
there would "guard, by its own means, against the
establishment of any future European colony within
its borders." The advice and documents which he
tendered were referred to the Committee of the
Senate on Foreign Relations. Its report, issued after
three weeks' deliberation, condemned the mission, and
at the same time severely handled the Monroe Doctrine. It was inexpedient, the Committee argued, for
the United States to join in an American congress to
prevent further colonisation on their continent. Their
people needed no help in guarding their own territories
against violation ; and they would refuse to guarantee
the dominions of foreigners. They would not deviate
from neutrality, nor engage in war to check the interference of any other power in the conflict between

Spain and the new states. Wider issues they condemned without mercy. The Government of the
United States could neither take part in forming a
continental system nor in negotiating for the settlement of "either principles of internal policy, or mere
abstract propositions, as parts of the public law."
Europe, they feared, would resent any such attempt to
benefit America at her own expense.

In March 1826, however, a small majority of the
Senate negatived the report of its Committee, and
upheld the action of the President.   His next step
was to send a Message in which he argued that the
conference would be a harmless and useful meeting
of diplomatists.   The "course of reasoning equally
simple and conclusive" which condemned future
European colonisation in America had never, he asserted, been contested by Russia, and had received the
entire assent of most of the new republics.   The latter
now proposed to consider "the means of making
effectual the assertion of that principle, as well as
the means of resisting interference from abroad, with
the domestic concerns of the American Governments."
What follows affords valuable evidence of the interpretation which the author of the Doctrine placed
upon it.   As to any conventional engagement, he
repeats, "our views would extend no further than to
a mutual pledge of the parties to the compact, to
maintain the principle in application to its own territory, and to permit no colonial lodgements, or establishments of European jurisdiction, upon its own soil."   The
United States, in effect, while refusing to guarantee
the territories of their neighbours, would in no degree

abandon their freedom to defend their own 'rights and interests,' when impugned by colonisation elsewhere.

The second principle of the Monroe Doctrine—that the United States could not behold with indifference any extension to America of the political system of the Allies—was also translated into action. "With respect to the obtrusive interference from abroad," the President continued, "if its future character may be inferred from that which has been, and perhaps still is, exercised in more than one of the new states, a joint declaration of its character and exposure of it to the world, may be probably all that the occasion would require. Whether the United States should or should not be parties to such a declaration, may justly form a part of the deliberation." In Adams's opinion, then, the Monroe Doctrine, while tolerant of monarchy in America, declared that the United States were interested in opposing any attempt on the part of Europe to introduce it by force or by intrigue. This interpretation, while it broadens the political horizon of the Doctrine, shows still more clearly its lack of legal form or nature. No one could suppose that the United States were *bound* to interfere, if an European power should violate the independence of a southern republic.

The remaining paragraphs of the Message labour to show that, since the establishment of the Constitution, America had acquired a set of primary interests of her own, with which, on the principle of reciprocity, Europe must not interfere. The acceptance of the invitation, therefore, while it could give no just cause of umbrage to the Holy Alliance or to Spain, was in harmony with the Farewell Address of Washington and with the Message of Monroe.

The policy thus defended was long and earnestly debated by the House of Representatives. The Opposition showed a strong desire to strip the Monroe Doctrine of its mystery. Loose notions of it, they urged, were misleading the representatives of the United States abroad, and must not be allowed to confuse the discussions at Panama. Did the United States intend, or did they not, to oppose European colonisation on the American continent? Were they prepared, or were they not, to resist any power but Spain which should interfere with the South Americans? They should not pledge themselves to the new Republics to do either the one or the other. Even a declaration that each power would maintain the principle of non-colonisation in application to its own territory would be inconvenient, since it would pledge the United States to make good their title to all the territory which they claimed. Any pretence to a kind of political supremacy over the whole continent might be dismissed as absurd.

Arguments like these stirred Daniel Webster to take up arms for the Doctrine as Adams had set it forth. The declaration against colonisation he justified by the commercial interest which rendered it highly desirable that the new states should adopt the principle of forbidding it within their respective territories. That against "a combination of the Allied Powers, to effect objects in America," he regarded as designed to preserve the rights of the United States. It neither

pledged them to remonstrate against a European inter-
dict of trade with the new states, nor to fight against
the Allies on behalf of provinces so distant as Chili
or Buenos Ayres.   An invasion of the shores of the
Gulf of ,Mexico, on the other hand, would present a
real danger, and would call for their decided and
immediate interference.   To him, the Monroe Doctrine
was a declaration of policy which a special crisis had
evoked.   It had done its work, and no fear of armed
intervention remained.   It would be expedient for the
United States, he argued, to similarly announce in
advance their intention, based on the right of self-
preservation, to resist the transference of Cuba to any
other power.   After long debate, the House resolved
that the people should be "left free to act, in any
crisis, in such manner......as their own honour and
policy might at the time dictate."   Clay's instructions
to the envoys destined for Panama, therefore, were
negative in tone.   Any joint declaration on the subject
of colonisation was not to bind the powers to maintain
the particular boundaries which might be claimed by any
one of them ; nor were they to be committed to resist
in common any future attempt to plant a new colony.

Such was the part played by the Monroe Doctrine
in discussions which might seem to the Spanish-
Americans part of a policy designed to frustrate their
effective union.   The envoys of the United States
reached Panama only to find that the Congress, after
effecting little, had adjourned.   It had been shown,
however, that the principles of 1823, successful in
attaining the political end for which they were announced, had gained credit with a large portion of the

nation. There was no sign, on the other hand, of general veneration for the Doctrine as an entity. Monroe himself was spending his last days in urging the Government to satisfy his pecuniary claims. The citizens of the United States might or might not share the antipathy of the Administration to European colonisation and political ideas. They showed clearly, however, that they were determined to avoid entangling alliances, and to plunge into the whirlpool of South American affairs only when and how they pleased. " No heated question," wrote a contemporary, "ever cooled off and died out so suddenly and completely."

CHAPTER IX.

LATER APPEALS TO THE MONROE DOCTRINE.

THREE years later, in 1829, Adams was thrust from office by Andrew Jackson, and the generation of statesmen which had given birth to the Monroe Doctrine passed from power. Problems of finance threatened to cleave the Union asunder, and all domestic questions began to be confused with that of slavery. After forty years of debate, the gigantic convulsion of the Civil War brought about Abolition. The nation was reconstructed, and a new era of industrial development began. Throughout the last seventy years of United States history, however, as in the half-century which has already been reviewed, the power and population of the Republic have increased without a check. They have been accompanied by a substantial extension of its territorial boundaries. The Monroe Doctrine was addressed to less than eleven million citizens. Twenty years later the total had well-nigh doubled. Federals and Confederates together numbered some 32,000,000; and in the three decades which have elapsed since the War, the population has swelled to at least 70,000,000.

Monroe spoke to twenty-four States; Cleveland to forty-four.

Much of this growth has been due to the advance of civilisation towards the West. The steady policy of the Administration, however, has been to expand the territory of the Union. Disputes as to its northern limits have resulted in the addition of a substantial area to its acknowledged dominions. By war and by purchase, Mexico has been induced to cede vast provinces on the south and west; and the acquisition of Alaska from Russia has enlarged the dominion on the Pacific. Development in the New World has been accompanied by peace with the Old. Save for an occasional deviation, such as that which resembled intervention in favour of the revolted Hungarians, the Republic has steered its course by the chart which Washington and J. Q. Adams marked out. At the outbreak of the Civil War, Lord Russell acknowledged the existence of a kind of understanding by which the United States abstained from European alliances, so long as European powers abstained from interference in American affairs. At the same time, the increase of population and the development of the means of transport have consolidated America, and lessened by four-fifths its distance from Europe. The people, ever mightier in numbers, can communicate in a few hours with the Administration, and, through the Administration, with the Cabinets of Europe.

Throughout this period of progress and development the popular will has remained supreme. On a continent doomed to geographical isolation, the United States are immeasurably the strongest power. Right or wrong, they can bear down the opposition of all the nations of America. The people know, too, that within their vast possessions their own will is law. In dealing with Europe, owing to the policy of which the Monroe Doctrine perpetuates the tradition, they stand steadily on the defensive. Thus, while invincible in their own hemisphere, they escape the mutual concession of European diplomacy. As against their own Government, their neighbours and Europe, they are wont, therefore, to gain every point upon which they insist. Hence they must inevitably tend to exalt their own authority, and to believe that their will has only to manifest itself to be obeyed. Such a people, it is clear, cannot be fettered by ancestral maxims which do not commend themselves to their present judgment. If the course recommended by a particular Executive officer falls into disfavour, none are more able or more ready to point out his lack of authority to bind his successor. Political creeds, again, can seldom be applied literally for many years. In the United States, even political parties become distinguishable by persons rather than by principles. The words of a declaration devised to meet Russia and the Holy Alliance, therefore, will be of small use when the Ukase has been withdrawn and the Alliance dissolved. From the time when its pro-mulgators went out of office, the Monroe Doctrine, if heeded at all as a canon of policy, must from the nature of the case have been applied with progressive meaning. It is an error to cite it as law, or to suppose that the collective will of the United States can impose rules upon the family of nations. To apply the formula of 1823 to the problems of a later age will probably be an error also. Whatever conclusions successive generations may draw from it, however, they possess increasing power to enforce. The Monroe Doctrine becomes the more dangerous, the less it is understood. The remainder of the essay, therefore, will be an endeavour, without ignoring the larger questions involved, to discover and to illustrate the political principles which Americans have regarded as its applications.

For two decades after the Panama Congress, the Monroe Doctrine slept. The attention of the United States was not distracted from domestic finance by any attempts to plant new colonies in America, or to extend to the New World the political system of the Old. The confederations of South America fell asunder, and many of the new governments were recognised by Spain. Their revolutions, however, disillusionised their northern admirers, and blighted the idea of a definite continental system under the hegemony of the United States. Their own rights being secure, the latter looked on unmoved while England and France mediated between southern powers, sent squadrons to enforce their claims, and exercised to the full the rights of their colonial empires. Meanwhile, in the case of Texas, the principle that the inhabitants of every territorial area may choose their own government was being strained in favour of the Union. In spite of the strenuous opposition of Adams, the drama of West Florida was being repeated on a grander scale. The President was arguing that Texas was practically a part of the United States ; and that it must be annexed to prevent the intervention of foreign powers. Then, if ever, there was need of some pretext of destiny or natural law to help out a doubtful case. The Monroe Doctrine, it might have been thought, lay ready to hand. Yet in the Message of April 22nd, 1844, it is ignored, if not violated, by the President. "The Executive," he says, "saw Texas in a state of almost hopeless exhaustion, and the question was narrowed down to the simple proposition whether the United States should accept the boon of annexation on fair and liberal terms, or, by refusing to do so, force Texas to seek refuge in the arms of some other Power, either through a treaty of alliance, offensive and defensive, or the adoption of some other expedient which might virtually make her tributary to such Power, and dependent upon it for all future time."

His successor, however, having been elected to acquire the province, turned the Monroe Doctrine to good account. M. Guizot had used expressions in the Chamber of Deputies implying that the annexation would disturb a balance of power on the continent of America. At the same moment, Great Britain was preferring her claim to the north-western—or Oregon —territory. In December, 1845, therefore, President Polk joined battle on both issues. The former he denounced as an European interference on the North American continent, such as the United States could not in silence permit, and such as they would be ready to resist at any and all hazards. "We must ever maintain the principle," he declared, "that the people of this continent alone have the right to decide their own destiny." Against the latter, since he assumed that the title of the United States to all the disputed territory was "clear and unquestionable," he quoted the principle of Monroe condemning European colonisation.

"This principle," he stated, "will apply with greatly increased force, should any European power attempt to establish any new colony in North America It should be distinctly announced to the world as our settled policy that no future European colony or dominion, shall, with our consent, be planted or established on any part of the North American continent." The Message forms a landmark in the history of the Monroe Doctrine. As a young opponent of Adams, Polk had regarded the paragraphs of 1823 as the mere expression of the opinion of the Executive, which had influenced the Holy Alliance, and thereby performed their office. He now, though ready to avail himself of the veneration due to the public opinion of the past, clothes its principles in a modern dress. He limits the Doctrine to North America, and pledges the United States to resist its violation. Above all, he extends the prohibition from colonisation to 'dominion.' The United States, if their President might speak for them, would never acknowledge any transfer of territory, whether made by the desire of the inhabitants, by purchase, or by force, from any nation of North America to any nation of Europe.

Polk thus began in 1845 the practice of claiming the authority of Monroe for whatever might be laid down as the current application of his principles. As tending to promote historical modes of thought and a coherent foreign policy, this might be advantageous. It was evil, however, in so far as it invited the people to believe that in their international relations they possessed rights greater than those to which, by International Law, they were entitled. In imitating Monroe,

succeeding Presidents might consult the best interests
of the Union. In using his name to cut knots which
without it baffled them, they were far from being his
imitators.

Six weeks later, a motion was made in the Senate
to endorse Polk's principles by resolution. Any attempt
to make an English colony of California was indicated
as falling under the ban. Like all other endeavours of
Congress to formulate the Monroe Doctrine, however,
that of 1846 was never completed. The Oregon question
was compromised ; and, after a series of military successes
against their neighbours, the United States retained
Texas, and purchased New Mexico and Upper California.
In 1848, the President further illustrated his Doctrine
against colonisation. Yucatan, which had been regarded
as a province of Mexico, was driven by an Indian re-
bellion to offer its sovereignty to the United States,
Great Britain and Spain in turn. Polk thereupon recommended its occupation by the United States, since
they "could not consent to a transfer of this 'dominion
and sovereignty' to either Spain, Great Britain or any
other European power." States in North America, in
effect, were free to determine their destiny so long as
it led them to join the Union. Events forbade the
occupation, but the Monroe Doctrine had received an
interpretation which could never have been put upon it
by its author.

The great problem of the control of the communication between the Atlantic and the Pacific by way of
Central America now came into prominence. Its connection with the Monroe Doctrine has been perhaps the
least obvious and the most important of the applications

of the Message of 1823 to subsequent affairs. Immediately after the United States had acquired California, they heard with indignation that Great Britain had seized territory in Central America which would give her the control of the proposed canal across the isthmus. The wrath of the people was heightened by the charge that she had absorbed the whole of Spanish Guiana. The Administration, however, when called upon to vindicate the Monroe Doctrine, disclaimed any pretension "to regulate all the affairs of this continent, so far as respects Europeans." With the sovereign rights of other nations over their existing colonies, said the Secretary of State, Monroe and Polk had assumed no right to interfere. "Such an assumption would have been equally obtrusive and ineffectual." Two years later, the question of interoceanic communication was settled for the time being by a convention known as the Clayton-Bulwer Treaty. The United States and Great Britain agreed to renounce any exclusive control over any route of transit that might be constructed from sea to sea, and solemnly debarred themselves from all fortification or dominion in Central America.

Meanwhile, the problem of insular Spanish-America had once more become prominent, and was now closely connected with the question of slavery. Great Britain and France had taken strong measures to check the American freebooters in Cuba, and in 1851 and 1852 they endeavoured to induce the United States to join them in guaranteeing the island to Spain. The answers of Daniel Webster and of his successor in the Department of State, without appealing to the Monroe

Doctrine, held firmly to the principle which it expressed. The United States, they declared, had no designs on Cuba, and would even support the Spanish dominion in the island. They were resolved, however, to avoid European alliances. The question was American, and of immense importance to the United States. They would continue, therefore, to oppose any attempt on the part of Spain to transfer the island to any European power. It was doubtful whether the Constitution would permit any Administration to renounce for all time the right of the United States to acquire Cuba by purchase, by war with Spain, or by the demand of its inhabitants acting as an independent nation. The European powers replied by an assertion of their own interest in the question, and of their entire freedom of action. They thus prevented any shadow of International Law from gathering round the extension to islands of dicta dealing with the mainland. The United States, however, had declared to the world that Cuba was as important to them as an island in the Thames or the Seine to England or France, and that their policy would attest the fact.

A new attempt, on the other hand, to formulate and endorse the principle on which their action would be based had proved a failure. In January 1853, Senator Cass had moved a resolution condemning in the language of the Monroe Doctrine as extended by Polk the establishment of any future European colony or dominion on the North American continent. The United States, according to his motion, regarded it as due to the vast importance of Cuba to declare "all efforts of other powers to procure possession, whether peaceably or forcibly, of that island, as unfriendly acts, directed against them, to be resisted by all the means in their power." The debate that followed led to no result. The question of Cuba, however, interwoven as it was with the question of slavery, continued to occupy the attention of the United States. The succeeding President, aiming at preventing Emancipation by annexing the island, endorsed the Monroe Doctrine in his Message of 1853. Next year, the Ambassadors of the United States to London, Paris and Madrid met at Ostend, and astounded Europe by a manifesto. If Spain refused to sell Cuba to the Republic, they declared, all laws divine and human would justify the Republic in taking it by force. In 1856, Cass argued that while Monroe's denunciation of interference with the Spanish colonies was obsolete, his declaration against colonisation was addressed to all nations and intended to operate during all time. It was founded on the situation of the United States, which demanded the system of separation advised by Jefferson. "This great Cis-Atlantic principle," he summed up, in words which may well be quoted, "does not derive its strength from its origin or its author; it rests upon a surer foundation, upon the cordial concurrence of the American people, and is destined to be a broad line upon the chart of their policy." Two years later, as Secretary of State under the feeblest of Presidents, it fell to his lot to broaden this line in checking Spanish intervention in Mexico. The United States, he instructed the Minister at Madrid, would not permit the subjugation by European powers of any of the independent states of that continent, nor would they

suffer Europe to exercise a protectorate over those
states, nor even to employ any direct political influence
to control their policy or their institutions.

The adherents of slavery, then, used the growing
strength of the Republic to thunder forth Polk's version
of the Monroe Doctrine.   Enlarging the principle of
non-colonisation, they strove to turn the balance of
parties in their own favour by forbidding Europe to
bring freedom to territories which might be annexed
to the South.   The prestige of a glorious past and
the patriotism of a vigorous present were thus identified
with the policy which Adams had combated to his
grave.   With the Northerners, therefore, the Doctrine
was in bad repute; and when in power, they were
reluctant to appeal to it.   Hence it came about that
in the only set of circumstances which represents a
distinct attempt on the part of Europe to extend its political system across the Atlantic, the Federal Government and its supporters refused to point their weapons
with the phrases of Monroe.   It becomes unnecessary,
therefore, to trace in detail the opposition of Secretary
Seward to the French intervention in Mexico during
the Civil War.   The proceedings by which Louis
Napoleon set up the throne of Maximilian, if not
"interposition for the purpose of oppressing" a government acknowledged by the United States, aimed
without doubt at controlling the destiny of a Spanish-
American nation.   His letter to the general in command, indeed, proved that the Emperor was aiming
at the establishment of French influence in the heart
of America.   France would be the loser, he showed,
if the United States should acquire the Gulf of Mexico,

dominate the West Indies and South America, and gain a monopoly of the products of the New World. His supporters might argue that it was the general interest of Europe to oppose a barrier to the imminent invasion of the whole American continent by the United States. In England, some rejoicing over the extinction of the Monroe Doctrine found public expression. Texas, the Confederates believed, was to be torn from them by France.

The establishment upon their borders of a government with objects such as these rendered it superfluous for the United States to justify opposition by any formula of policy. It may be maintained, indeed, that Seward's despatches when his country seemed on the verge of ruin were written in a different spirit from those which were dictated by an enormous and high-spirited army. It may be equally true that by continuing to regard Mexico as a republic when all Europe recognised it as a monarchy, by refusing to acknowledge a blockade in actual operation, and by secretly supplying the opponents of Maximilian with arms, the United States departed from neutrality. The words in which the American Secretary of State developed his views, moreover, hinting as they do at a republican intervention against monarchical ideas, may be condemned as contrary to the Law of Nations. The fact none the less remains that, in driving the French from Mexico, Seward relied on the principle of national independence alone. From lawfully prosecuting her claims, he told Napoleon, France had diverged into a war of intervention. She was maintaining by force a government contrary to the true desires of the Mexican people. Every power, as a member of the international police, has the right to interfere in behalf of any nation which it may deem to be oppressed. To gain a right of counter-intervention, therefore, the United States, if sincere and well-informed, had no need to allege, as their official friendship for France prompted them to do, that the new government in Mexico was by nature antagonistic to themselves.

Their citizens, however, had not been equally philosophic. All the skill of the Secretary of State had been taxed to avert a war. Public opinion was expressed in April, 1864, when the House of Representatives unanimously declared that it was not fitting for the people of the United States to acknowledge any monarchical government, erected on the ruins of any republican government in America, under the auspices of any European power.

This disposition to champion republicanism, repressed in the original Monroe Doctrine, discernible in the despatches of Seward, and shouted aloud by Congress, was strengthened by the victory of the North. The United States, though devoted to the institutions which they have devised, seem always to have been sensitive to the opinion of their European critics. At the close of the Civil War, they were still the only great nation of modern times which had created a permanent republic. France had twice abandoned monarchy, and as often resumed it. It was impossible even for a parent to look with pride on the governments of Spanish-America. Republicanism, though acquiesced in, remained on its trial, and there was still a note of defiance in the tone of its pioneers. The authors of the Monroe Doctrine, it was true, had decided that they could not frown officially on monarchy in Brazil. As the Old World became more tolerant of republicanism, however, the New World became more intolerant of monarchy. Men strove to base their instinct on principle, and turned to the vague phrases of 1823. It has not been the least of the errors surrounding the original Monroe Doctrine, to term it an anathema against kingship in America.

These feelings found utterance when, in 1866, the House of Representatives considered a bill for the eventual annexation of the continent north of their own borders. They were answered by the British North American Act, which united Canada, Nova Scotia, and New Brunswick into a single Dominion. This constituted the sharpest check which the development of the Monroe Doctrine had received. Though it violated no formula of the American people, it was in conflict with their belief that Canada was destined speedily to become their own, and showed the impotence of such statements as Seward's declaration that " British Columbia, by whomsoever possessed, must be governed in conformity with the interests of her people, and of society upon the American continent." The measure, none the less, was too clearly within the rights of Great Britain to form a legitimate grievance against her. The House of Representatives could only declare the uneasiness of the United States at witnessing such a vast monarchical conglomeration of states on their frontiers, in contravention of their traditionary and constantly declared principles.

The fourteen years which followed were for America

years almost without a history. With the accession of
Garfield to power, however, the Monroe Doctrine was
again brought into prominence. Blaine, the new Secretary of State, vetoed as inadmissible the guarantee
by European powers of the neutrality of the Panama
Canal. The new waterway, he argued, would be the
great highway between the Atlantic and the Pacific
States of the Union, and would thus substantially form
a part of its coast-line. Its control, therefore, must be
in the hands of the United States. Such a claim, it
was evident, came into conflict with the Clayton-Bulwer
treaty concluded between the United States and Great
Britain in 1850. The gist of that agreement had been
that, in order to remove international difficulties, both
parties abjured dominion in Central America. To
comply with it, Great Britain had made sacrifices which
had caused the President, in 1860, to congratulate
Congress on " a final settlement entirely satisfactory to
this Government." To this settlement she now adhered, in spite of Blaine's suggestions that the treaty
should be modified in favour of the United States. To
decide the case, the American public appealed to the
Monroe Doctrine. The declaration against colonisation
was interpreted as forbidding any European power to
gain a footing on the American continents, either by
colonisation, intrigue, or commercial autocracy. The
denunciation of any attempt on the part of the Old
World to extend its political system to the New, was
made to condemn the influence in Central America
which the canal would give to its possessors. All the
words of Monroe, it was maintained, justified the United
States in declaring the agreement void.

During the first sixty years of its existence, then, the Monroe Doctrine had been cited in cases which varied much, but which possessed one feature in common. In all of them, the interests or security of the United States were at stake. Their people had increased in power, and in feelings of hostility to American monarchy; while there had always been an undercurrent of sentiment in favour of a loose protectorate over the republics of the South. Such a political relation, however, had never been asserted or assumed. The action of Great Britain, alone, had constantly disproved it. With Adams in power, she had established the Republic of Uruguay. Despite the outcry of the Argentine, she had occupied and retained the Falkland Islands. Andrew Jackson had refused to check her territorial aggression, though Central America implored him to interfere. She had at different times enforced her claims against Southern States by intervention, embargo, reprisals and blockade, without arousing the protest of the Executive at Washington. France, Spain, and the United States themselves had followed her example. South Americans, indeed, have bitterly complained that their northern brethren forget their mission to protect them, and that the gun-boats of Europe exact from them indemnities at will.

Recently, however, what may prove to be a new chapter in the history of the Doctrine seems to have been begun. For the first time, the Administration has shown some readiness to adopt the popular view which sees a violation of the Monroe Doctrine in every British movement in the New World. In 1895, Great Britain exacted a fine from Nicaragua for outrages

upon her subjects. A section of the people of the
United States at once cried out that the Monroe
Doctrine had been violated, but President Cleveland,
in his annual Message to Congress, approved the act.
A fortnight later, however, he roused the whole Union
to fury by alleging that Lord Salisbury's refusal to
submit to arbitration a boundary dispute with Venezuela had violated the principles of Monroe. The facts
upon which this allegation was based, as presented in
Mr Olney's despatch of July 20th, involve an elaborate
treatment of the Doctrine as applied to South America.
Venezuela, says the Secretary of State, in the course
of a long-standing boundary dispute with Great Britain,
had frequently appealed to the Government at Washington to take cognisance of the injury of which she
complained. So early as 1881, his predecessor had
assured her of the deep interest felt by the Administration "in all transactions tending to attempted en-
croachments of foreign powers upon the territory of
any of the republics of this continent." Continuing
to watch the progress of events with friendly interest,
and at times with grave concern, the United States
had vainly offered their mediation, and had pressed
Great Britain to appoint an arbitrator. Her determination to adhere at all costs to a portion of the
territory which she claimed, however, caused them now
to declare the controversy one in which their honour and
interest were involved, and the continuance of which
they could not regard with indifference.

To prove this proposition, Mr Olney took the
unusual course of appealing to the Monroe Doctrine by
name in negotiating with a foreign power. Almost one

half of his voluminous despatch consists of an account of the origin and history of the Message of 1823, and of an argument that its principles extend to the existing dispute. The Doctrine itself he regards as a form peculiarly and distinctively American of the admitted canon of International Law that a nation may intervene between two parties, when the act of either is a serious and direct menace to its own integrity, tranquillity or welfare. Its formulation by Monroe supplemented the Farewell Address of Washington "by declaring in effect that American non-intervention in European affairs necessarily implied and meant European non-intervention in American affairs." Such a rule the United States alone were competent to enforce. Monroe, therefore, courageously declared that any European power so interfering would be regarded as antagonising their interests and inviting their opposition.

The rule itself, in no way establishing a protectorate, has, he contends, but a single object. "It is that no European power or combination of European powers shall forcibly deprive an American state of the right and power of self-government, and of shaping for itself its own political fortunes and destinies." "That the rule thus denned has been the accepted public law of this country ever since its promulgation," he quotes history to show. He seems to approve the declaration of Secretary Bayard that the United States are "the peculiar guardians" of the rights of the New World. From the facts cited, he concludes "that the Venezuelan boundary controversy is in any view far within the scope and spirit of the rule as uniformly accepted and acted upon." The material and moral interests of

Europe, he urges, are "irreconcilably diverse from those of America; and any European control of the latter is necessarily both incongruous and injurious." Resistance to it must come from the United States, whose safety and welfare are "so concerned with the maintenance of the independence of every American state as against any European power as to justify and *require*" their interposition whenever that independence is endangered. To reject this proposition would be to sacrifice the advantages resulting to themselves from the proximity, sympathy. and republicanism of the remaining nations of America. Their resources and isolated position, again, have made them "practically sovereign" on that continent, and their fiat law upon the subjects to which they confine their interposition. This superiority would vanish if the principle were admitted that European powers might convert American states into colonies or provinces of their own. Europe might then partition out the countries of the South, and militarism would be thrust upon the New World. To abandon the Monroe Doctrine, therefore, would be to renounce a policy which has proved both an easy defence against foreign aggression, and a prolific source of international progress and prosperity. Its application to the boundary dispute between Great Britain and Venezuela, he maintains, presents no real difficulty. Important political control is in dispute—to be lost by one party and gained by the other. Great Britain cannot be deemed a South American state within the purview of the Monroe Doctrine. Hence the case falls under the inhibition of 1823, and the United States are entitled and required to interfere. Much more, then, have they the right to demand that the facts on which their interference must be based, should be determined.

The argument of this despatch, endorsed by the President in his special Message of December 17th, pledges the Administration to a view of the Monroe Doctrine which is in reality new. In his opinion, said Mr Cleveland, it would be the duty of the United States to resist by every means in their power, as a wilful aggression upon their rights and interests, the appropriation by Great Britain of any lands, or the exercise of governmental jurisdiction over any territory, which, after investigation, they had determined of right to belong to Venezuela. This conclusion, if approved by the nation, would measure the progress of the Doctrine during seventy-two years. Where Monroe spoke of "the manifestation of an unfriendly disposition," Cleveland would read "wilful aggression upon rights and interests." The United States, according to the former, "could not behold such interposition with indifference," while the latter deems it their duty to resist by every means in their power.

It seems difficult, however, to understand the argument that the interests of the United States were connected with the question actually at issue. If action were taken, it must be on account of an obligation to enforce the letter of the Monroe Doctrine. The new departure in practice, then, was accompanied by a new departure in theory. The United States, in the opinion of the Administration, must interfere, not because morality prompted them to succour the oppressed, nor even in obedience to any appreciable demands of the

law of self-preservation, so much as because a principle
of policy formulated by a long-dead President might
be construed as requiring them to take a given course.
Foreign powers, they held, must accept the Monroe
Doctrine as binding the Federal Executive to make
demands, just as it had been previously claimed that
the Constitution forbade them to yield to demands of
others. Their policy, while it delighted America,
astounded Europe. Lord Salisbury, in his reply to the
American despatch, denied that the Monroe Doctrine
was either a rule of International Law or a formulation
of principles applicable to the present dispute. The
British nation as a whole expressed the same belief.
The European press protested against the assumption
by the United States of authority over a whole hemisphere. The interests of European, as opposed to
American, civilisation in the New World were held to
be at stake. The United States, it was feared, could
not claim to exercise a protectorate over their southern
brethren without assuming the responsibility which
such a relationship must imply. The alarm was heightened by rumours of a proposed congress of South
Americans to endorse the Monroe Doctrine, and to
place themselves under the hegemony of the United
States.

The European attack upon the Monroe Doctrine
was valuable as tending to divest it of its disguise as a
part of International Law. Of more importance was
the action of the United States. In spite of the
criticism of their publicists, East and West joined in a
paroxysm of enthusiasm for a doctrine of which a
hundred conflicting explanations were on their lips.

The Senate, almost by acclamation, approved of the commission advocated by the President for the investigation of the British claim ;—a measure which to English eyes seemed "perhaps the most astounding proposal advanced by any government in time of peace since the days of Napoleon." Once more an attempt was made to induce the Legislature to formulate and endorse the Monroe Doctrine, and once more the result was failure. The revised text, drafted by a Senator, would have particularly condemned any attempt by any European power to add to its territory or sovereignty on the American continent or islands by " force, purchase, cession, occupation, pledge, colonisation, protectorate, or by control of the easement in any canal or any other means of transit across the American isthmus."

When such views as these found support in the Legislature, it is not surprising that less responsible citizens went to great lengths. One result of the gigantic controversy, indeed, was to show the world that the United States, as a nation, give the Monroe Doctrine a prominent place in their political creed. In a people whose great lack is the want of common questions, it thus tends strongly to promote unity. Another gain was the demonstration that moderate interpretations of the Doctrine would command the sympathy of Great Britain, whose desire, as her Premier in effect conceded, was not to enlarge her possessions, so much as to develop them. Many of the American interpretations, however, could not be termed moderate. "The grab-all policy of England," wherever possible, was brought under the ban. Men were found to assert that the South Americans might not cede their territories

10—2

to her against the interests of the United States, and that her dominion in Canada was unnatural and inexpedient. The United States, others argued, ought to fulfil the Monroe Doctrine by requiring every dispute between a European and a South American power to be settled by arbitration. Perhaps the clearest indication of its growth, however, was furnished by its popular application to Cuba. The Cabinet of Monroe had expressly declined to assist the islanders in insurrection. Seventy years later, they had rebelled without more apparent justification. Many Americans, none the less, believed that the Monroe Doctrine commanded the United States to attack Spain in order to give Cuba independence.

To reject the proposition that the United States are compelled by any doctrine or traditional policy to take action which their present interests do not require, only common sense is needed. That any such doctrine or policy can warrant them in action which, apart from it, would be condemned by International Law, has already been disproved. Wherever their own interests are reasonably affected, or their conscience outraged, they, like any other power, have the right to interfere. Their private political traditions neither augment nor diminish that right. Attention may be profitably directed, however, to the tendency, implied though disavowed, of the United States to quote the Monroe Doctrine in assuming a loose protectorate over the nations of South America. The causes of this tendency may be read in the text and between the lines of Mr Olney's despatch. "Distance and three thousand miles of intervening ocean," lie at the base of the whole.

Having postulated the separation of America from Europe, it is not difficult to concede that the fiat of the United States becomes law in the Western hemisphere. Its advantages to themselves, and indirectly to the world, are obvious. Their international position is simplified, their ambition gratified, and their blood and treasure spared. At first sight, therefore, this rendering of the Monroe doctrine finds much to recommend it. It is impossible, however, to ignore its bearing on the future. Hitherto, the internal development of the Union has been favoured by the existence of relatively inexhaustible supplies of land. With fertile territories crying out for settlement, a foreign policy has been superfluous. It requires no gift of second-sight, none the less, to predict that this good fortune cannot, under existing conditions, last for ever. Reasons for acquiring possessions outside their present boundaries must tend to arise with increasing force. It is the duty, therefore, of all states which esteem the right of national independence, and the interest of all which have colonial possessions in the neighbourhood of the United States, to examine the foundations of a Doctrine which would lead the Government at Washington to assume special powers over an entire hemisphere.

To destroy the idea that there is a natural separation between European and American States is to shatter the key-stone of the whole. It is impossible, indeed, to argue away the Atlantic Ocean. But it is equally impossible to ignore the existence of electricity and steam. The relations between Europe and Asia, and between North and South Africa, prove that land, rather than water, separates one nation from another. With existing means of transit, men journey between London and Washington with greater speed and safety than between Washington and Mexico or Lima ; and it is difficult to understand why the Isthmus of Panama should bind the interests of South to those of North America. It is the intercourse of nations, rather than their geographical position, that determines the rules prevailing between them. If Europe and America are connected by real and important relations, it is vain to deny that those relations are controlled by law. Distance and three thousand miles of intervening ocean could shut out the Law of Nations only if they cut off international communication.

There is reason to believe, therefore, that the geographical distance of America from Europe is not sufficient to give the United States any special right to regulate the affairs of their own hemisphere. It may further be questioned whether, Europe apart, the Southern nations would accept even such political control on the part of the United States as is implied in the suggestion that they exercise in America a hegemony like that of the Great Powers in Europe. To such a modification of the doctrine of the equality of states, there are, indeed, grave objections. A single power, however strong its moral sense, is not compelled to distinguish duty from interest as clearly as is a member of a group of six endeavouring to induce the others to join it in concerted action. The nations of South America would, no doubt, sacrifice much to gain the United States as an ally. They would be untrue to their Spanish ancestors, on the other hand, if they accepted her protection at the price of any portion of their political independence. Their publicists and people alike, while desiring to stand apart from Europe, seem to reject the idea of inferiority, and to display no general affection for the United States. In climate, in race, in civilisation, and in religion, Anglo-Saxon and Latin America are hopelessly diverse. " We should derive no improvement to our own institutions," prophesied J. Q. Adams, "by any communion with theirs," and the prophecy has been fulfilled. The Constitution of the United States, both in letter and in spirit, forbids the Executive to assume anything like a protectorate over a continent. It would be impossible, moreover, for a group of sovereign states in the South to accept the habitual control of a federation of sovereign states in the North. It would be equally impossible to derive from a Doctrine aimed at confirming the independence of Spanish-America any warrant for overthrowing it. Between politically controlling the southern states, and treating them as entirely independent, there is no middle course, and the Monroe Doctrine cannot find one.

In its latest development, then, as throughout its history, the Doctrine has induced confusion of thought. The flood of sentiment and rhetoric poured out on both sides of the Atlantic has in great part obscured the truth. It has served, none the less, to establish the position of the Monroe Doctrine as a political force, which—however esteemed—must be recognised. Above all, by the Old World and the New, it must be understood.

APPENDIX.

Spanish-America in relation to the Monroe Doctrine.

The nine governments to which the rule of Spanish-America had been originally entrusted seem, by their hostility to progress, and by their oppression of the native Indians, to have justified the rhetoric which has been poured forth against them. In each, authority was in the hands of a caste of colonial Spaniards, and each was an isolated entity, communicating only with Spain. The younger Pitt, and his successor, had endeavoured without success to strike a blow at the ally of France by encouraging her colonies to revolt. Loyal till loyalty became impossible, they showed the bitterest resentment of the slur cast by Napoleon upon their mother-country. The course of events in the Peninsula, however, forced them to set up Juntas of their own, and their alienation from Spain was completed by the massacres with which the movement was opposed. In July, 1811, Venezuela declared its independence, to be followed by Mexico and New Granada, and, in 1813, by Buenos Ayres. Having achieved its own deliverance, the last-named sent its army to free Chili also, and in 1817 succeeded in there subverting the royal power. Meanwhile the most violent fluctuations had marked the progress of revolution in Mexico, New Granada and Venezuela. The bloodiness with which the armies of Spain carried out the principle that their opponents were traitors rather than belligerents established an uncompromising hatred of Spanish and even of monarchical rule. At last, led by Bolivar, and stimulated by the constitutional victory in the mother-country, the forces of South American liberty triumphed; while Mexico, though divided and thrown back by the usurpation of Iturbide, had likewise cleansed herself from foreign domination. Central America followed their example, and at the same time a different course of events had severed the empire of Brazil from the crown of Portugal.

As the confusion of revolt had abated, it had become evident that the realm of Ultramar had split into seven chief fragments. At the mouth of the Rio de la Plata, Buenos Ayres gave its name to a loose federation of fourteen provinces, of which it was the chief. Mr Woodbine Parish, despatched thither as British Commissioner in 1824, reported that the total population of the league was less than one million. Independence, actually enjoyed since 1810, had been formally declared in July 1816. It had recently been confirmed by the interchange of Ministers with the United States, and recognition by Great Britain would crown the work. The people were unalterably resolved not even to discuss any remaining pretensions of Spain, and they had rejected four several propositions for the restoration of a Bourbon rule. Their chief foreign relations were with the other revolted states of South America; and by a domestic law they had undertaken to join them in a compact to make no treaty with the mother-country until she had recognised all as independent. Whatever may have been their esteem for the United States, to whom they owed their model of government and its first acknowledgment, their language showed that they looked rather to Great Britain for international establishment and protection. The Secretary for Foreign Affairs, advancing against Canning's suggestion of favour to Spanish commerce the argument that "Spain could hardly expect exclusive privileges from the enjoyment of which the natives themselves were debarred," was careful to add that "they were sincerely disposed to enter into any arrangement with His Catholic Majesty's government upon such terms as Great Britain would say were fair and reasonable." The Minister to the United States was despatched by way of England. Another distinguished revolutionist had been allowed to leave the country only under a solemn promise to take no step towards altering the constitution without first securing the advice and approval of the British Government. In spite of the system of schools and universities on which the President could congratulate the nation, and in spite of the social refinement which captivated the British Commissioner, it was to England that the children of high officials were sent for education. In matters the most important and the most trivial the Ministers of Buenos Ayres were eager to fulfil every wish of the power which might, as they hoped, "succeed in obtaining peace for South America," and from which they desired intervention even in their boundary disputes with Brazil. And when at last Great Britain had granted the boon of recognition, their representative was instructed to express the warm gratitude "common to all classes in his country" for "the political transactions which have fixed the destiny of these provinces."

Paraguay, the province through which flows the chief of the rivers which join the Atlantic at Buenos Ayres, need be mentioned only to be dismissed. Its Dictator surpassed the exclusiveness of Spain by cutting off all communication between his country and the world outside, and the climate combined with Jesuit discipline to enforce his will. Foreigners might enter the country, but none were permitted to leave it. For thirty years, therefore, his dominions were, for international purposes, blotted from the map of South America.

Columbia, less favoured than Buenos Ayres in the easy attainment of its independence, was a federation of the States now known as Venezuela, Columbia and Ecuador. British possessions, therefore, in the shape of Guiana and the West Indies, were much less distant from its borders than was any sphere of influence of the United States. The fact which J. Q. Adams admits, moreover, that South America needed the products, not of the North, but of England, sufficiently indicates the relative commercial weight which the two countries might be expected to enjoy. Sentiment and interest seemed to be on the same side. The citizens of the United States, though American, were as truly foreign as the British. The people were devoted to their President Bolivar, and the flower of Bolivar's troops were subjects of George III. Hence, though the agents of the Republic held different language to different powers, and though the British Commission of 1824 misused its opportunities, it seems possible to accept the verdict of one of its members that all parts of Columbia showed stronger feelings of attachment to Great Britain than to the United States. The latter, it was true, in Columbia also had been the first to recognise a government modelled on their own. They had not, however, gained certain exclusive privileges which they were supposed to have requested as a reward. To Great Britain, on the other hand, the Columbians were ready to offer, as the price of recognition, a law which should withhold such privileges from all powers which did not similarly acknow-

ledge them.   Here, as in Buenos Ayres, moreover, distrust
of France prevailed.   Powerless at sea, Columbia trusted
in Great Britain to check the allies of Spain.   Against
Spain unaided, however, Columbia could more than hold
her own.   Her army under Bolivar was the salvation of
Peru, and it was to her that the states of Latin America
looked for guidance into the path of union.

The zone of country which separated Columbia from
Buenos Ayres was occupied by the republic of Peru.   Of
its political and social condition, at a time when the
Royalists were still in the field, the British Commissioner
draws a vivid picture.   " The present bayonet," he says,
" is the present god here."   All estates are ruined.   Any
independent Peruvian government it is difficult to find.
External relations, therefore, were of the slightest.   In so
far, however, as the Peruvians could see the world outside,
they, like their opponents, seem to have looked to England
rather than to the United States.   The meagre news-sheet
of the country found space for the Parliamentary speeches
of Liverpool and Lansdowne.   The royalist press, on the
other hand, derided the hopes of its adversaries that their
liberty would be preserved by ' La política Europea,' and
traced them to a rumour that England was about to send
commissioners to South America.   These facts, coupled with
the prevalent silence as to the United States, confirmed
the report that "all parties in Peru appear to want the
influence, mediation or *power* of friends in Europe to be
exerted for them."   The Royalists might look to France
or Russia; the party of independence, only to Great Britain.

Of Chili, a long strip of territory between the southern
Andes and the sea, the British Government could obtain
little information.   The scanty reports of envoys sent in
1824 proved only that the country was entitled to small
military or commercial consideration.   It seemed doubtful

whether the insurgents could drive out the Royalists, or themselves resist attack from Europe. The soil, indeed, was fertile, but the people poor and lazy. " All the population west of the Andes, from Cape Horn up to the Mexican coast, is not equal in number to that of the line of five miles or six drawn round St Paul's," wrote the British Consul-General in Peru. Chili had concluded treaties with Columbia, Buenos Ayres and Peru, and faintly echoed the cry for a closer union. Here, again, the agents of France seem to have been at work, but their secret offer of mediation with Spain, if made, was declined by the young republic. The United States had been the first power to establish a consulate in the country, and they maintained a small squadron in the Southern Pacific. Great Britain, on the other hand, was represented by a colony of merchants, and the South American policy of her government gave general satisfaction. It seems idle to draw political inferences from such facts as these.

At the time when the Monroe Doctrine was promulgated, then, Spanish South America lay in a rude crescent round the western and southern boundary of the Guianas and Brazil, countries which for more than a century and a half had been dependencies of Europe. Guiana remains to this day subject to France, Holland and Great Britain. The huge territory of Brazil, on the other hand, with an area of more than three million square miles, had in 1822 quietly severed its government from that of Portugal. Having become an independent empire under a sovereign of the House of Braganza, its example might encourage the powers of Europe in their endeavours to accommodate actual facts to their Legitimist theories. Colonies which rejected even the nominal sovereignty of Spain might, Chateaubriand hoped, accept a monarchical form of government under princes of the house of Bourbon. The internal state of the new empire, however, seems to have been comparable with that of Peru and Chili, while hundreds of miles of forests shut off communication with its neighbours on the map. Between Spaniard and Portuguese, moreover, there was nothing but hatred, and the remaining members of the South American family must be sought beyond the Isthmus of Panama.

The institutions of the united provinces of Central America, otherwise known as Guatemala, presented a striking likeness to those of Columbia and Buenos Ayres. While the bulk of the people looked on with indifference, their leaders had formed a loose federation, and had striven to imitate the political system of the United States. They were conscious, however, of a weakness which their sister federations were slow to acknowledge. " Although," writes the British Commissioner, "the Guatemalians seem naturally to want less the protection of some European power than most of the other independent colonies of the same hemisphere, they do in fact solicit it more than any other." After prior relations with the United States, and a rumoured application for admission to the Union, the power to which they turned was Great Britain. It would be vain, indeed, to look to Guatemala—a temporary collection of some two million inhabitants, for any marked individual influence on the politics of the world at the era of the Monroe Doctrine. The frankness with which it threw open to foreigners the commerce and citizenship of all its provinces entitles it, none the less, to an honourable mention among the new republics. None of them marked more clearly its improvement on the political system of the mother-country.

Most northerly of the revolted Spanish dominions was the federal republic of Mexico. Including, besides its present territory, what now constitutes some eight of the United States, it embraced, according to its representatives in England, an area five times as great as that of Spain. Its position as a member of the South American system was defined in an early treaty with Columbia. By this both powers bound themselves to defend their independence against the world, and to endeavour to bring the other states of Spanish-America into that compact of " perpetual union, league and confederacy " which was to be sealed by a general assembly at Panama. The British Commissioners who arrived at the close of 1823 found that thirteen years of war had desolated the country, and that many among the clergy, nobility and army, encouraged by French intrigues, were in favour of a monarchy. Spain alone, however, as the governor of her remaining island-fortress admitted, could prevail neither by conquest nor conciliation. Mexico might reward her immediate recognition with commercial privileges, but would decline to purchase it. She would look to England not merely for recognition of independence, but also for protection against foreign aggression. The United States, the only commercial rivals of Great Britain, had at the close of 1823 no accredited Minister residing in her dominions; and though they had ventured much capital in the country it had not bought them the favour of the inhabitants. Canning held, indeed, that the two states were too neighbourly to be friendly. Distressed and divided, the Mexican federation could exercise little influence beyond its own borders. The weight of evidence tends to show however that—as in all the more considerable of the republics—her respect and interests alike turned rather to Great Britain than to any other power.

Such, then, was the political condition of the American continents south of the United States at the period of the Monroe message. One common sentiment inspired all the former dominions of Spain—a resolution " To lay waste the country and destroy the towns rather than permit the reentrance of the Spaniards." In all else the several communities were less homogeneous than distant observers might imagine. The governments, much less the people, of Mexico and Guatemala could know little of Chili and Peru. The press was of the feeblest; and public opinion, then as now, withered beneath the suns of the tropics. The states were loose confederations of provinces, and their population composed of the most motley elements. Its ignorance of the world at large was only equalled by the ignorance of the world concerning it. At a capital so near as the Havana, the accounts received of the mainland were so vague and contradictory as to render it extremely difficult to judge of passing events. Despatches of the Columbian commissioners reached England in three months, while those from Peru might take four. It was the British representative in Chili who established a weekly communication with Buenos Ayres; and his colleague in Buenos Ayres who secured a monthly communication with Great Britain. The mixed origin of the population, and the lack of manufactures and common interests, joined with climate and tradition to prevent anything like Spanish-American concert. Of this the self-isolation of Paraguay, unchecked for thirty years, is in itself sufficient proof.

Except when fighting against Spain, therefore, Spanish-America was little more than a geographical expression. The mother-country, even when constitutional, proclaimed that its peoples were incapable of governing themselves. Peninsular history since the beginning of the century might incline the world to believe her. "The Spanish character," owned king Ferdinand's premier to the ambassador of Great Britain, "could not maintain a very long struggle against the energy, activity, and enterprise of the race that sprung from the British Isles." With some show of reason, however, he maintained that its peculiarities were beyond the comprehension of British commissioners. The men, perhaps not altogether disinterested, who now reported that Spanish-America was irrevocably constitutional might, he insinuated, be as mistaken as those who four years before had said the same of Spain in Europe. What the mother-country lacked in force, he insisted that she might accomplish by moral influence. A royal army need only appear in South America and offer commercial privileges, to rally round its banners an immense party of the discontented. "With the cord of St Francis on one side, and the cordon and star of Isabella the Catholic on the other, we shall do more," said Monsieur Ofalia, "than with all the armies we could send out. These are ties not easily to be broken." Even apart from conciliation, he maintained, the revolution was unpopular. The rebel nations, in effect, were neither rebellious nor national. Peace commissioners sent to Guatemala, Mexico and Columbia had failed, but he declared that "the highest and the lowest classes throughout the country were in favour of a re-union with Spain. The middling classes were perhaps against it." A fortnight later, he could report that "with the exception of the lawyers (perhaps *en masse*) and a few discontented physicians," all South America was in favour of accommodation.

For the governments that claimed the obedience of the people, Spain had nothing but contempt. "What is the present state of South America," the representative of the Cortes at Washington had asked, "and what are its governments, to entitle them to recognition?" Disunion and despotism, every loyal Spaniard would reply, and men outside the Peninsula believed him. Three years earlier, Bagot had left Washington in doubt as to whether the insurgents would ever establish permanent governments. In 1823 Polignac maintained that they had made no progress. With Spain this belief was a fixed principle which no evidence could assail. While Ofalia acknowledged as notorious "the fact that no Spanish army could be trusted,—almost every officer employed in America had passed over to the side of the insurgents," his master defied the representatives of the Allies to make him listen to reason. The people were equally deaf to all save their own prejudices. The press breathed no surrender, and called on Spain to consolidate her triumphs in Peru, to support her handful of brave men in Costa-Firma, and to plant the pennons of Castille on the towers of Mexico. Neither king nor people however, could subdue America of themselves. The mediation of Great Britain, which the Spaniards would have preferred to any other, could only be procured by recognition. France refused to listen to their request for armed intervention. Only the Czar and the Holy Alliance remained. Constitutional Spain had appealed to Europe to do nothing that could prejudice her cause. Monarchical Spain, by inviting her allies to Paris, begged her to make her cause her own. The answer to the invitation had been sealed at Washington, and was already in Canning's hands.

CAMBRIDGE: PRINTED BY J. AND C. F. CLAY, AT THE UNIVERSITY PRESS.

RETURN TO: CIRCULATION DEPARTMENT
198 Main Stacks

LOAN PERIOD	1	2	3
Home Use			
	4	5	6

ALL BOOKS MAY BE RECALLED AFTER 7 DAYS.

Renewals and Recharges may be made 4 days prior to the due date.
Books may be renewed by calling 642-3405.

DUE AS STAMPED BELOW.

DEC 2 0 2000		
	.	

FORM NO. DD 6
50M

UNIVERSITY OF CALIFORNIA, BERKELEY
Berkeley, California 94720–6000

Printed in Great Britain
by Amazon.co.uk, Ltd.,
Marston Gate.